Contract
BRIDGE
Summary

ALBERT H. MOREHEAD
Editor

William Root
Technical Consultant

The Macmillan Company, New York

Acknowledgment is made to the following books for material based on them.

The Laws of Contract Bridge, 1963, © by American Contract Bridge League.

Point-Count Bidding (also, *Contract Bridge Complete* and other books) by Charles H. Goren.

Contract Bridge Complete (also, *Culbertson's Own Summary* and other books) by Ely Culbertson.

Bridge Is a Partnership Game, by Alvin Roth and Tobias Stone.

How to Play Winning Bridge, by Edgar Kaplan and Alfred Sheinwold.

The Complete Stayman System of Contract Bidding, by Samuel M. Stayman.

The Club Convention System of Bidding at Contract Bridge, by Harold S. Vanderbilt.

Better Bidding in 15 Minutes, Expert Bidding in a Week, by Howard Schenken.

Blueprint for Bidding, by J. Terence Reese and Albert Dormer.

The Quintessence of CAB, by Ewart Kempson and Norman de V. Hart.

The Complete Italian System of Winning Bridge, by Edgar Kaplan.

The Roman Club System of Distributional Bidding, by Giorgio Belladonna and Walter Avarelli.

The Bridge World, published in New York by A. Moyse, Jr.;
Contract Bridge Bulletin, published in New York by American Contract Bridge League; and many other bridge periodicals published throughout the world.

First Printing

Printed in the United States of America

The Macmillan Company, New York
Collier-Macmillan Canada, Ltd., Toronto, Ontario

Library of Congress catalog card number: 63-20922

HOW TO USE THIS SUMMARY

This Summary is a quick reference book for bridge players. It is designed to tell, at a glance:

1. What you need for any bid.
2. What you should bid with the hand you hold.
3. What you should lead when it is your turn.
4. How you should play certain combinations of cards.
5. How to interpret the special systems and the many bidding conventions that are most popular.

Since the Summary gives this information, automatically it tells what you should expect your partner to have when he makes any bid, lead, or play.

In the opening pages, which present bidding information that will cover at least 95% of all bidding situations, this book is based on the Goren System. However, mention is made of certain modifications which, in conjunction with the Goren System, make up the system usually called Standard American. These opening pages also fairly represent the Culbertson System, on which the Goren System was based, subject to such developments as have occurred since the late Ely Culbertson wrote his last books.

The index on the inside back cover will help you find the precise information you are seeking on any particular bid, lead, system, or convention. The thumb-indexing arrangement will give quick access to any general topic covered in this book.

HOW TO USE THE THUMB-INDEX

Hold all the pages between your right thumb and forefinger, with your thumb on the subject you wish to find. Release the pages slowly until the black section is under your thumb. (You will probably detect the section you seek from the black edges you see when you fan the pages.)

POINT-COUNT VALUATION

BIDDABLE SUITS

OPENING ONE-BIDS

CHOICE OF SUITS

FORCING BIDS

RESPONSES TO SUIT-BIDS

OPENER'S REBIDS

RESPONDER'S REBIDS

NOTRUMP BIDDING

OPENING 3, 4, 5 BIDS

FORCING TWO-BIDS

OVERCALLS

TAKEOUT DOUBLE

PENALTY DOUBLES

PART-SCORE

DUPLICATE

SLAM BIDS

4-5 NOTRUMP SLAM BIDS

BIDDING CONVENTIONS

PERCENTAGE TABLES

BIDDING SYSTEMS

OPENING LEADS

SIGNALS IN PLAY

COVERING HONORS

FINESSES

SAFETY PLAYS

END-PLAYS SQUEEZE

BRIDGE LAWS

GLOSSARY

POINT-COUNT VALUATION

Before bidding, count the number of points in your hand. High-card points control notrump bidding; both high-card and distributional points are counted when you bid a suit.

THE NOTRUMP POINT-COUNT

Ace	4
King	3
Queen	2
Jack	1

ADD 1 point if you hold all four Aces

DEDUCT 1 point for an aceless hand, or for King singleton or Q-J doubleton

These are the only points counted for notrump opening bids.

POINT-COUNT FOR OPENING SUIT-BIDS

I. COUNT OF HIGH-CARD POINTS

Same as at notrump: 4,3,2,1

(Including 1-pt. addition for four Aces and deduction for an aceless hand, King alone, or Q-J alone.) Also,

ADD 1 point for 100 honors in a suit and **2 points** for 150 honors.

II. COUNT OF DISTRIBUTIONAL POINTS

To your high-card point total,

When bidding your own suit, add:
1 point for each doubleton
2 points for each singleton
3 points for each void

For raising partner's suit, add:
1 point for each doubleton
3 points for each singleton
5 points for each void

The extra points for short suits when raising may be added only if you have adequate trump support.

DEDUCT 1 point if you have only 3-card trump support, no matter how high (or low) the cards.

DEDUCT 1 point if you have 4-3-3-3 distribution.

The count of a hand is calculated by adding together its high-card and distributional points.

HOW HIGH TO GO IN BIDDING

There are 40 points in the deck. The side that has the majority of these points is usually able to make some contract.

The average hand is 10 points.

Each bid promises some minimum number of points. Add your points to the minimum partner has shown by his bidding. Depending on the combined total, you should bid (or invite, or force) a final contract according to the following table.

POINTS HELD IN COMBINED HANDS	TRICK EXPECTANCY
20 to **24**	PART-SCORE ZONE. Pass as soon as a safe contract is reached (unless partner's last bid was forcing).
25	NEAR-GAME ZONE. Game possible in good-fitting major or at notrump.
26	GAME ZONE. Bid game in major with 8 combined trumps, or at notrump.
29	GAME in minor suit (often safer than notrump), but prefer major suit.
33	SLAM ZONE—investigate controls for small slam (page 60).
37	GRAND SLAM ZONE—investigate both first- and second-round controls (pages 60-67).

MATHEMATICS OF GAME BIDDING. Game should be bid with about a 50% chance to make it when not vulnerable, with slightly less (about a 45% chance) when vulnerable. *Unless you go down about once in three or four game tries, you are underbidding.*

POINT-COUNT
VALUATION

BIDDABLE
SUITS

OPENING
ONE-BIDS

CHOICE
OF SUITS

FORCING BIDS

RESPONSES
TO SUIT-BIDS

OPENER'S
REBIDS

RESPONDER'S
REBIDS

NOTRUMP
BIDDING

OPENING
3, 4, 5 BIDS

FORCING
TWO-BIDS

OVERCALLS

TAKEOUT
DOUBLE

PENALTY
DOUBLES

PART-SCORE

DUPLICATE

SLAM BIDS

4-5 NOTRUMP
SLAM BIDS

BIDDING
CONVENTIONS

PERCENTAGE
TABLES

BIDDING
SYSTEMS

OPENING
LEADS

SIGNALS
IN PLAY

COVERING
HONORS

FINESSES

SAFETY PLAYS

END-PLAYS
SQUEEZE

BRIDGE LAWS

GLOSSARY

3

QUICK TRICKS or HONOR TRICKS

Nearly every bid requires some minimum number of quick tricks, which are cards or combinations of cards that may be expected to win tricks no matter what the final contract is—whether at notrump or in a trump suit, whatever suit is trump, and whether your side plays it or the opponents play it.

An opening bid always requires 2 quick tricks in at least two suits, and usually 2½ or 3 quick tricks or more.

Quick tricks are often called *defensive tricks*, because they will win even in defense against opponents' bids; or *honor-tricks*, but some combinations of cards that are called honor-tricks are not quick tricks. Only the following cards or card combinations are quick tricks.

QUICK TRICKS	
IF YOU HAVE	**COUNT**
A-K in the same suit	**2** quick tricks
A-Q* in the same suit	**1½** honor-tricks
Ace **K-Q** in the same suit **K-x and K-x†**	**1** quick tricks
K-x† **Q-J-x***	**½** quick tricks

A hand may be well above average in points but lack enough quick tricks to warrant a bid:

♠ K-Q-10-6-3   ♥ K-J-5   ♦ Q-J-7-4   ♣ 3
    5   4   3   2

This hand has 14 points, counting the singleton club, but has only 1½ quick tricks (♠ K-Q and ♥ K) and should not be bid originally.

---

*The ½ quick trick counts only if the hand has more than 2 quick tricks.
†The symbol "x" means any lower card in the suit.

4

POINT-COUNT
VALUATION

BIDDABLE
SUITS

OPENING
ONE-BIDS

CHOICE
OF SUITS

FORCING BIDS

RESPONSES
TO SUIT-BIDS

OPENER'S
REBIDS

RESPONDER'S
REBIDS

NOTRUMP
BIDDING

OPENING
3, 4, 5 BIDS

FORCING
TWO-BIDS

OVERCALLS

TAKEOUT
DOUBLE

PENALTY
DOUBLES

PART-SCORE

DUPLICATE

SLAM BIDS

4-5 NOTRUMP
SLAM BIDS

BIDDING
CONVENTIONS

PERCENTAGE
TABLES

BIDDING
SYSTEMS

OPENING
LEADS

SIGNALS
IN PLAY

COVERING
HONORS

FINESSES

SAFETY PLAYS

END-PLAYS
SQUEEZE

BRIDGE LAWS

GLOSSARY

BIDDABLE SUITS

A biddable suit is a suit that may be bid if the hand as a whole is strong enough. Partner should expect that the suit contains at least four cards and at least 4 points in high cards (for example, K-J-x-x or A-10-x-x).

For opening suit-bids, a major suit should usually be either a *strong* 4-card suit or a 5-card or longer suit. A minor suit may be weaker and when necessary (to avoid bidding a weak major suit) may even be a 3-card suit—see *The Short Club,* page 76.

For responses at the one-level, or for rebids at the level of one or two, either a major or a minor suit may be weaker but should be at least 4 cards in length.

If possible, avoid bidding a suit headed by less than A, K, or Q, so as to be able to stand an opening lead in the suit if the opponents play the hand.

HOLDING	WHEN TO BID IT
K-x-x-x **Q-10-x-x** (4 cards) up to K-J-x-x or A-10-x-x **x-x-x-x-x** (5 cards) or better	*In minor suits,* may be bid at the one-level, in opening or responding, and at the two-level in rebidding. *In major suits,* may be bid only in responding or re-bidding at the one-level. Should not be rebid unless partner has raised TWICE.
Q-J-x-x up to A-K-Q-J **Q-x-x-x-x** (any 5 cards) or better	May be bid in a major or minor suit, in opening, re-sponding, or rebidding, at the one- or two-level, but should not be rebid unless partner has raised.
x-x-x-x-x-x (any 6 cards) **K-J-x-x-x** **Q-J-9-x-x**	**REBIDDABLE SUITS** May be bid in any suit, in any circumstances, and may be rebid (once) if necessary, but no suit weaker than A-J-10-x-x or K-Q-10-x-x or Q-J-x-x-x-x should be rebid
K-Q-J-x-x-x (6 cards) **Q-J-x-x-x-x-x** **K-x-x-x-x-x-x**	May be bid and rebid *twice* (or at the three-level) with-out support, if the hand as a whole is strong enough.

5

WHEN TO OPEN THE BIDDING

1. Count your high-card points. Without at least 10 pts. in high cards you should rarely open the bidding.

2. Look for 2 quick tricks. With less, you should not open with a one-bid.

3. Look for a biddable suit. Without one, you should not open without at least 14 pts.

4. Make an opening bid, vulnerable or not, first, second, third or fourth hand, if your *high-card* points and *quick tricks* conform to the following table.

Weaker hands may be opened in third position, if the suit bid is strong and the bidder wishes his partner to make the opening lead in that suit.

IF YOU HOLD	WHAT YOU SHOULD DO
10 points or less	PASS. *Exception:* A shut-out bid on a 7- or 8-card suit. See also page 7.
11 points	BID a 6-card *major* suit. (You must have at least 2 quick tricks, with ½ trick outside the trump suit.) *Bid one spade:* ♠ K-Q-8-6-5-2 ♡ 10-7 ◇ A-9-4 ♣ 6-3 PASS with less.
12 points	BID any rebiddable suit. (You must have at least 2½ quick tricks, with ½ trick outside the trump suit.) *Bid one spade:* ♠ A-K-8-5-4 ♡ K-9-7 ◇ Q-6-4 ♣ 8-3 PASS with less.
13 points	BID any biddable suit. *Bid one diamond on:* ♠ 8-6-4 ♡ A-K-2 ◇ K-J-8-6 ♣ K-4-3 *or* ♠ A-6 ♡ 10-9-5 ◇ K-7-6-4-3 ♣ A-Q-3
14 to **18** points	DO NOT PASS. BID ANY BIDDABLE SUIT. BID ONE NOTRUMP with balanced distribution (page 33).
19 points or more	PREFER an opening suit-bid unless your hand justifies a two-bid (page 44) or two-notrump bid (page 33).

WHEN TO OPEN THE BIDDING

There are two schools of thought in American bidding, those who open the bidding "light," for example on

♠ 8-6-4   ♡ A-K-2   ◇ Q-10-6   ♣ K-8-4-3   Bid 1 ♣

and those who prefer "sound" (strong) opening bids and would pass such a hand. Either approach can be effective. The majority prefer to open light, but perhaps 1 or 2 pts. stronger than the hand shown.

Anticipation, or **Principle of Preparedness.** An opening bid should not be made in any circumstances unless the bidder is prepared to rebid safely, and without misrepresenting his hand, over any one-round-forcing response his partner may make. A rebid of two notrump, any reverse bid (page 26), and any raise of partner's suit to three, even when it is not a jump raise, shows a strong hand—16 pts. or more. Therefore an opening bid should not be made unless the bidder can make a weak-sounding rebid (one notrump, a suit rebid that is not a reverse, or a single raise of the responder's suit to *two*) or unless the bidder's hand is strong.

♠ K-6   ♡ J-10-5-2   ◇ 7-4   ♣ A-K-10-6-5

Bid one club. Over a response of 1 ◇ or 1 ♠ the rebid will be 1 N.T. Over a response of 1 ♡ the rebid will be 2 ♡.

♠ J-5-4-3   ♡ A-6   ◇ A-Q-10-6-3   ♣ J-6

Bid one diamond. Over a response of 1 ♡ the rebid will be 1 ♠. Over a response of 1 ♠, the rebid will be 2 ♠. Over a response of 2 ♣ the rebid will be 2 ◇.

♠ A-Q-7-6   ♡ 6-3   ◇ K-Q-8-2   ♣ J-7-3

Pass. If 1 ♠ were bid, there would be no safe rebid over a 2 ♡ response; if 1 ◇ were bid, there would be no rebid over 2 ♣ that would not misrepresent either the strength or the distribution of the hand.

Third- and Fourth-hand Bids. When partner has passed originally, his suit response to an opening bid is *not forcing*. The bidder needs the same number of points for an opening bid but does not have to worry about his rebid because he is permitted to pass. The hand last cited above should be opened with a one-spade bid and any nonforcing response should be passed.

Weaker major suits, or weaker hands, may be opened in third or fourth positions. After two or three passes, the following may be good bids.

♠ Q-J-6-5   ♡ A-4   ◇ 10-9-7-3   ♣ K-Q-8

Bid one spade. In first or second position the bid (if the holder bids at all) should be one club.

♠ 6-3   ♡ K-Q-10-8-6   ◇ 8-5-4   ♣ A-7-2

Bid one heart, third hand; pass in any other position.

WHICH SUIT TO BID FIRST

With two biddable suits, at least one of which is a 5-card or longer suit, it is usually correct to bid first *the longer suit when they are not of the same length and the higher-ranking suit when they are equal in length,* even if the suit that is not bid first is considerably stronger than the other.

An exception is made by many players with a 5-card spade suit and another 5-card suit that may be stronger, *when the spade suit is not rebiddable:*

♠ Q-8-7-5-3	♡ A-3	♢ 7	♣ A-Q-10-7-6	One club
♠ K-J-10-7-6	♡ K-3	♢ 7	♣ A-J-10-5-4	One spade
♠ 7	♡ Q-8-7-5-3	♢ A-Q-10-7-6	♣ A-3	One heart
♠ 10-8-6-5-2	♡ A-K-8-6-3	♢ A-9	♣ 4	One heart

WITH TWO BIDDABLE SUITS

Divided	Your Choice Should Be
5-5 or **6-6**	Bid the higher-ranking. *Bid one spade on:* ♠ Q-8-5-3-2 ♡ A-K-Q-4-3 ♢ 9-2 ♣ 9 or ♠ 10-8-6-4-3-2 ♡ — ♢ A-K-10-7-3-2 ♣ 8
5-4 With 18 or more pts.	Bid the longer suit first. *Bid one diamond on:* ♠ A-K-Q-4 ♡ 8-3 ♢ A-K-9-6-5 ♣ 7-2
5-4 With 17 pts. or less	Bid the higher-ranking when the suits are *"touching"* in rank. Bid the longer suit when they are *not touching.* *Bid one spade on:* ♠ A-J-8-4 ♡ A-9-7-5-2 ♢ K-10-4 ♣ 6 *Bid one club on:* ♠ 9-5 ♡ A-K-7-3 ♢ Q-6 ♣ K-J-8-5-4
6-5	Bid the longer suit first, then bid the shorter suit TWICE. *Bid one diamond on:* ♠ A-J-5-3-2 ♡ 10 ♢ K-Q-10-7-4-3 ♣ 6 or ♠ A-Q-8-7-4-2 ♡ — ♢ K-9-8-7-6-4-3 ♣ —
7-6	Bid the higher-ranking.
6-4 or **7-5**	Bid the longer suit TWICE, then show the shorter suit *Exception:* When you can show the shorter suit by a rebid at the level of one. With ♠ 6-5 ♡ A-J-8-3 ♢ 4 ♣ A-K-9-7-6-2 Bid one club. If partner responds one spade, bid two clubs. But if partner responds one diamond, bid one heart.

8

CHOICE BETWEEN 4-CARD SUITS

As a simple rule that is easy to remember: With two 4-card biddable suits, one of which is clubs, bid **one club;** lacking a club suit, first bid the **higher-ranking** suit.

But no rule is perfect for this difficult choice. The following tables give advice that will provide safety in most cases. See also page 7.

YOUR SUITS	YOUR FIRST BID
4 Spades or Hearts **and** **4** Clubs	**ONE CLUB.** *Bid one club on:* ♠ A-K-8-4 ♡ 9-2 ◇ 8-6-3 ♣ K-Q-4-3 *or* ♠ 9-6 ♡ A-Q-J-5 ◇ Q-6-3 ♣ A-Q-8-2
4 Spades **and** **4** Hearts	**ONE SPADE.** *Bid one spade on:* ♠ K-Q-6-2 ♡ K-J-10-4 ◇ A-J-6 ♣ 8-4 *or* ♠ K-J-10-8 ♡ A-Q-6-5 ◇ 9-6-5 ♣ A-3
4 Hearts **and** **4** Diamonds	**ONE HEART.** *Bid one heart on:* ♠ 9-6 ♡ A-J-3-2 ◇ A-K-Q-8 ♣ 7-5-2 *or* ♠ A-K ♡ K-J-8-6 ◇ Q-J-4-3 ♣ 10-9-5
4 Diamonds **and** **4** Clubs	**ONE DIAMOND.** *Bid one diamond on:* ♠ 8-6-3 ♡ K-9 ◇ A-K-7-6 ♣ A-Q-9-4 *But with minimum hands bid one club:* ♠ 8-6-3 ♡ 10-7 ◇ A-K-7-6 ♣ A-J-9-4
4 Spades **and** **4** Diamonds	**Usually Bid the Stronger Suit** *but with support for hearts, bid one spade; with support for clubs bid one diamond. Bid one spade on:* ♠ K-J-6-4 ♡ Q-7-3 ◇ A-K-5-2 ♣ 4-3

═══ With 4-4-4-1 ═══

FIRST BID THE BIDDABLE SUIT next in rank *below* the singleton.

One spade	*One heart*	*One diamond*	*One club*
♠ A-J-5-2	♠ 9	♠ A-K-7-3	♠ A-9-7-2
♡ A-Q-6-4	♡ A-Q-4-2	♡ 9	♡ A-Q-8-4
◇ K-J-8-5	◇ K-Q-6-5	◇ K-8-5-4	◇ 8
♣ 6	♣ K-9-8-7	♣ K-10-7-6	♣ K-8-6-3

Five-card majors. In several systems and among many players, an opening bid may not be made on a major suit shorter than 5 cards, especially in 1st or 2nd position. The hands shown above would be opened:

♠ K-Q-6-2	♡ K-J-10-4	◇ A-J-6	♣ 8-4	Bid 1 ◇
♠ K-J-10-8	♡ A-Q-6-5	◇ 9-6-5	♣ A-3	Bid 1 ♣
♠ 9-6	♡ A-J-3-2	◇ A-K-Q-8	♣ 7-5-2	Bid 1 ◇

See also The Short Club, page 78

POINT-COUNT VALUATION
BIDDABLE SUITS
OPENING ONE-BIDS
CHOICE OF SUITS
FORCING BIDS
RESPONSES TO SUIT-BIDS
OPENER'S REBIDS
RESPONDER'S REBIDS
NOTRUMP BIDDING
OPENING 3, 4, 5 BIDS
FORCING TWO-BIDS
OVERCALLS
TAKEOUT DOUBLE
PENALTY DOUBLES
PART-SCORE
DUPLICATE
SLAM BIDS
4-5 NOTRUMP SLAM BIDS
BIDDING CONVENTIONS
PERCENTAGE TABLES
BIDDING SYSTEMS
OPENING LEADS
SIGNALS IN PLAY
COVERING HONORS
FINESSES
SAFETY PLAYS
END-PLAYS SQUEEZE
BRIDGE LAWS
GLOSSARY

BIDS THAT ARE FORCING
A. Game-Forcing Bids

A forcing bid is a demand to partner to keep the bidding open until you have had another chance to bid.

A jump' bid (one trick more than necessary) is usually *forcing to game*. Both partners must keep the bidding open until game is reached,* except that a penalty double of an opponent's bid may be passed.

The following bids are forcing to game; they are forcing for one round even when, with a part-score, they would be enough for game.

1. Any opening two-bid in a suit.† (An opening two-notrump bid is not forcing—page 33.)

SOUTH	WEST	NORTH	EAST	SOUTH	WEST	NORTH	EAST
Pass	Pass	2 ♢ (*Forcing*)		Pass		2 N T (*Not forcing*)	

2. A jump bid in a new suit (called a *jump shift*) provided partner has made an opening bid or responded to an opening bid.

SOUTH	WEST	NORTH	EAST	SOUTH	WEST	NORTH	EAST
1 ♡	Pass	3 ♢ (*Forcing*)		1 ♡	Pass	1 N T	Pass
		or 2 ♠ (*Forcing*)		3 ♣ (*Forcing*)			

3. A bid in the opponents' suit (cue-bid)—see pages 51 and 61.

SOUTH	WEST	NORTH	EAST	SOUTH	WEST	NORTH	EAST
1 ♡	1 ♠	2 ♢	Pass	1 ♡	Pass	1 ♠	2 ♣
2 ♠ (*Forcing*)							(*Forcing*)

The following jump responses to an opening bid are forcing to game **unless the responder passed originally.** They are not forcing when, with a part-score, game has been reached; but they are strength-showing bids and suggest a possible slam. They are limited bids, not as strong as the jump shifts shown above, and may be passed if the opener did not have a genuine opening bid.

1. A double raise in a major suit (page 15).
2. A jump response of two notrump (page 13).

SOUTH	WEST	NORTH	EAST	SOUTH	WEST	NORTH	EAST
1 ♡	Pass	3 ♡ (*Forcing*)		1 ♡	Pass	2 N T (*forcing*)	

SOUTH	WEST	NORTH	EAST	*North-South have 40 on score:*			
Pass	Pass	1 ♠	Pass	SOUTH	WEST	NORTH	EAST
3 ♠ (*Not forcing*)				1 ♡	Pass	3 ♡ (*not forcing*)	

*It is a bidding convention, not a law of contract bridge, that the bidding must be kept open to game after a forcing two-bid, or any other game-forcing bid. The partner should continue bidding but cannot be required to do so.

†Many experts use an opening two-club bid as an artificial game-forcing opening bid. See page 44.

FORCING BIDS (Cont'd)
B. One-round Forcing Bids

The following bids are forcing for one round; but not if the responder has passed originally, or if the response, with a part-score, is enough for game.

1. Any suit takeout of an opening suit-bid of one.

SOUTH	WEST	NORTH	EAST
1♦	Pass	1♠ (Forcing)	

SOUTH	WEST	NORTH	EAST
1♥	Pass	2♣ (forcing)	

SOUTH	WEST	NORTH	EAST
Pass	Pass	1♠	Pass
2♦ (Not forcing)			

North-South have 60 on score:

SOUTH	WEST	NORTH	EAST
1♥	Pass	2♦ (not forcing)	

2. Any new-suit *rebid* by the responding hand.

SOUTH	WEST	NORTH	EAST
1♦	Pass	1♣	Pass
2♦	Pass	2♥ (Forcing)	

SOUTH	WEST	NORTH	EAST
1♣	Pass	1♦	Pass
1♥	Pass	1♠ (Forcing)	

EXCEPTIONS: A new-suit rebid by the responding hand is not forcing if the opener's rebid was one notrump or if the responder's first response was one notrump.

SOUTH	WEST	NORTH	EAST
1♥	Pass	1 N T	Pass
2♣	Pass	2♦ (not forcing)	

SOUTH	WEST	NORTH	EAST
1♥	Pass	1♠	Pass
1 N T	Pass	2♣ (not forcing)	

A reverse new-suit rebid by the responder is one-round-forcing even if the opener's rebid was one notrump and is game-forcing if the opener made any other rebid.

SOUTH	WEST	NORTH	EAST
1♣	Pass	1♥	Pass
1 N T	Pass	2♠ (Forcing, one round)	

SOUTH	WEST	NORTH	EAST
1♦	Pass	1♥	Pass
2♦	Pass	2♠ (Forcing to game)	

Jump Bids That Are Not Forcing

The following jump rebids are always strength-showing but are not forcing if partner's previous bid showed weakness or possible weakness, such as a one-notrump response or one-over-one bid.

1. A jump rebid in notrump.
2. A jump rebid in the suit the player bid previously.
3. A jump raise in partner's suit.

SOUTH	WEST	NORTH	EAST
1♦	Pass	1♥	Pass
2 N T *or*			
3♥ *or* } Not forcing			
3♦			

SOUTH	WEST	NORTH	EAST
1♣	Pass	1♥	Pass
1♣	Pass	2 N T (Not forcing)	

SOUTH	WEST	NORTH	EAST
1♠	Pass	1 N T	Pass
3♠ (Not forcing)			

SOUTH	WEST	NORTH	EAST
1♠	Pass	1 N T	Pass
2♦	Pass	3♠ (Not forcing)	

The same bids are forcing if partner's previous bid showed strength, such as a two-over-one response to an opening bid (page 17).

SOUTH	WEST	NORTH	EAST
1♠	Pass	2♦	Pass
3♣ (Forcing)			

SOUTH	WEST	NORTH	EAST
1♦	Pass	1♠	Pass
2♦	Pass	3♣ (Forcing)	

RESPONSES TO SUIT-BIDS OF ONE

When your partner makes an opening suit-bid of one, and the next player passes,* respond as follows. The requirements given apply to *high-card points only*. More detailed information on pages 13 to 21, and on page 41 (sacrifice bidding), explain some exceptions in which distributional points may reduce the number of high-card points needed.

YOU HOLD	PROPER RESPONSE
0 to 2 pts.	PASS *Only exception:* Bid a 7-card *major* suit
3 or 4 pts.	USUALLY, PASS But bid ONE in a 6-card major suit
5 pts.	RAISE if able (see page 20) BID ONE in a 5-card suit (Bid one notrump with two suits stopped) Lacking these values, PASS
6 to 9 pts.	BID ONE in *any* biddable suit BID TWO in a 6-card suit RAISE with Adequate Support BID ONE NOTRUMP
10 pts.	BID ONE in *any* biddable suit BID TWO in a 5-card suit RAISE with Adequate Support BID ONE NOTRUMP
11 to 14 points	Bid any biddable suit Bid another suit first, if you have a fit with your partner's bid, and your hand is too good for a single raise (over 10 points); or not good enough for a double raise (13-16 points)
13 to 15 pts.	Double raise with 4 trumps (13-16 points) Show any biddable suit. Bid two notrump (13-15 pts.) Bid three notrump (16-18 pts.) with balanced distribution
16 pts.	Bid three notrump with 4-3-3-3 distribution in high cards Make a forcing takeout in another suit

*For *Free* Responses after a double or overcall, see page 21.
For responses over an opponent's takeout double, see page 55.

NOTRUMP RESPONSES

A notrump response usually shows a balanced hand (no singleton or void). It is strictly limited and at each level may be made with *no more and no less* than the strength prescribed below.

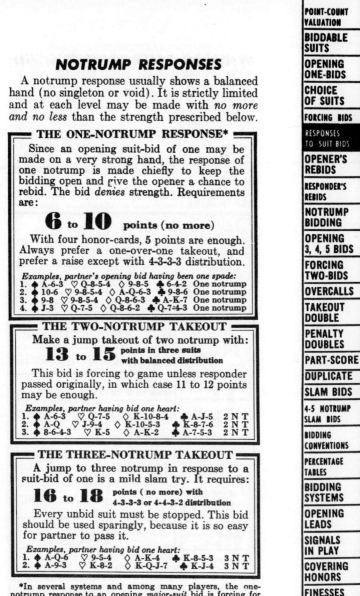

THE ONE-NOTRUMP RESPONSE*

Since an opening suit-bid of one may be made on a very strong hand, the response of one notrump is made chiefly to keep the bidding open and give the opener a chance to rebid. The bid *denies* strength. Requirements are:

6 to 10 points (no more)

With four honor-cards, 5 points are enough. Always prefer a one-over-one takeout, and prefer a raise except with 4-3-3-3 distribution.

Examples, partner's opening bid having been one spade:
1. ♠ A-6-3 ♡ Q-8-5-4 ◇ 9-8-5 ♣ 6-4-2 One notrump
2. ♠ 10-6 ♡ 9-8-5-4 ◇ A-Q-6-3 ♣ 9-8-6 One notrump
3. ♠ 9-8 ♡ 9-8-5-4 ◇ Q-8-6-3 ♣ A-K-7 One notrump
4. ♠ J-3 ♡ Q-7-5 ◇ Q-8-6-2 ♣ Q-7-4-3 One notrump

THE TWO-NOTRUMP TAKEOUT

Make a jump takeout of two notrump with:

13 to 15 points in three suits with balanced distribution

This bid is forcing to game unless responder passed originally, in which case 11 to 12 points may be enough.

Examples, partner having bid one heart:
1. ♠ A-6-3 ♡ Q-7-5 ◇ K-10-8-4 ♣ A-J-5 2 N T
2. ♠ A-Q ♡ J-9-4 ◇ K-10-5-3 ♣ A-J-5 2 N T
3. ♠ 8-6-4-3 ♡ K-5 ◇ A-K-2 ♣ A-7-5-3 2 N T

THE THREE-NOTRUMP TAKEOUT

A jump to three notrump in response to a suit-bid of one is a mild slam try. It requires:

16 to 18 points (no more) with 4-3-3-3 or 4-4-3-2 distribution

Every unbid suit must be stopped. This bid should be used sparingly, because it is so easy for partner to pass it.

Examples, partner having bid one heart:
1. ♠ A-Q-6 ♡ 9-5-4 ◇ A-K-4 ♣ K-8-5-3 3 N T
2. ♠ A-9-3 ♡ K-8-2 ◇ K-Q-J-7 ♣ K-J-4 3 N T

*In several systems and among many players, the one-notrump response to an opening *major-suit* bid is forcing for one round. See page 18.

POINT-COUNT
VALUATION

BIDDABLE
SUITS

OPENING
ONE-BIDS

CHOICE
OF SUITS

FORCING BIDS

RESPONSES
TO SUIT BIDS

OPENER'S
REBIDS

RESPONDER'S
REBIDS

NOTRUMP
BIDDING

OPENING
3, 4, 5 BIDS

FORCING
TWO-BIDS

OVERCALLS

TAKEOUT
DOUBLE

PENALTY
DOUBLES

PART-SCORE

DUPLICATE

SLAM BIDS

4-5 NOTRUMP
SLAM BIDS

BIDDING
CONVENTIONS

PERCENTAGE
TABLES

BIDDING
SYSTEMS

OPENING
LEADS

SIGNALS
IN PLAY

COVERING
HONORS

FINESSES

SAFETY PLAYS

END-PLAYS
SQUEEZE

BRIDGE LAWS

GLOSSARY

WHEN TO RAISE PARTNER'S SUIT

The following table gives requirements for raising partner's opening suit-bid of one.

Every raise requires *adequate trump support*.

Minimum adequate trump is shown in the left column below.

Usually prefer to raise a major suit but prefer a suit takeout—especially a one-over-one takeout—to a raise in a minor suit.

See more detailed explanation of raises on pages 15 and 16.

The point requirements in the following table include both high-card and distributional points.

HOLDING IN PARTNER'S SUIT	POINTS	WHAT TO DO
X-X-X-X-X [5 or more trumps] Powerful support. Raise as many times as the total strength of your hand justifies.	**6** to **10**	SINGLE RAISE
	8 to **10**	TRIPLE RAISE
	13 to **16**	DOUBLE RAISE
Q-X-X-X [4 trumps or better] Immediate support. Justifies three raises even if partner does not rebid the suit.	**6** to **10**	SINGLE RAISE
	11 or **12**	PREFER a suit bid
	13 to **16**	DOUBLE RAISE
X-X-X-X .4 small trumps or K-Q-x, A-Q-x, A-K-x Immediate support. Justifies two raises even if partner does not rebid the suit.	**6** to **10**	SINGLE RAISE
	11 or **12**	PREFER a suit bid
	13 to **16**	DOUBLE RAISE
J-10-x, Q-x-x or better. Adequate support. Do not raise more than once unless partner rebids the suit.	**9** or **10**	SINGLE RAISE But 4 trumps are needed to raise when partner has rebid in a new suit.
x-x-x or **Q-x** or better	Adequate trump support for a suit partner has rebid; or if his first bid was two or more in that suit. See also Preference Bids, page 31.	

14

RAISES OF PARTNER'S MAJOR SUIT

Situation: Partner has made an opening bid of one spade or one heart; the next player has passed. Prefer a raise unless you can make a two-over-one suit takeout (or a one-over-one in a fairly good spade suit). With a weak 4-3-3-3 hand prefer a one-notrump response.

POINT-COUNT
VALUATION

BIDDABLE
SUITS

OPENING
ONE-BIDS

CHOICE
OF SUITS

FORCING BIDS

RESPONSES
TO SUIT BIDS

OPENER'S
REBIDS

RESPONDER'S
REBIDS

NOTRUMP
BIDDING

OPENING
3, 4, 5 BIDS

FORCING
TWO-BIDS

OVERCALLS

TAKEOUT
DOUBLE

PENALTY
DOUBLES

PART-SCORE

DUPLICATE

SLAM BIDS

4-5 NOTRUMP
SLAM BIDS

BIDDING
CONVENTIONS

PERCENTAGE
TABLES

BIDDING
SYSTEMS

OPENING
LEADS

SIGNALS
IN PLAY

COVERING
HONORS

FINESSES

SAFETY PLAYS

END-PLAYS
SQUEEZE

BRIDGE LAWS

GLOSSARY

SINGLE RAISE OF A MAJOR

A raise of partner's major suit to two is not forcing. Partner is invited to pass unless he had a strong opening bid. The raise requires adequate trump support (page 14) and

6 to **10** points (no more)

With 5 trumps, 5 pts. are enough.

Examples, partner having bid one heart:
1. ♠ 6 ♡ 7-5-3-2 ◇ K-J-6-4 ♣ 7-5-4-3 Two hearts
2. ♠ K-6 ♡ Q-8-5-3 ◇ 9-6-5-2 ♣ Q-7-4 Two hearts
3. ♠ A-9-5 ♡ Q-J-3 ◇ 8-6-5 ♣ K-6-5-3 Two hearts
4. ♠ 6 ♡ 10-8-6-3-2 ◇ K-8-6-2 ♣ 8-5-4 Two hearts
5. ♠ A-10-6-5-3 ♡ Q-7-4 ◇ 8-6-2 ♣ 9-5 One spade
6. ♠ J-8-4 ♡ 8-7-5-3 ◇ A-7-6 ♣ Q-7-5 One notrump

DOUBLE RAISE OF A MAJOR

A jump raise of partner's major suit to three is *forcing to game,* unless the responder has previously passed. The bid requires:

IN TRUMPS: **Q-x-x-x, J-10-x-x,** or **x-x-x-x-x** (any 5 trumps)

13 to **16** points (no more) with at least 10 pts. in high cards

If the responder has previously passed, he may give a double raise with 11 or 12 pts.

Examples, partner having bid one spade:
1. ♠ K-J-9-7-6 ♡ 6-5-3-2 ◇ A-Q-J ♣ 7 Three spades
2. ♠ K-8-5-4 ♡ A-7-6 ◇ J-8-5-2 ♣ A-7 Three spades
3. ♠ 9-6-5-3 ♡ A-K-Q ◇ 7-5-4 ♣ A-6-3 Three spades
4. ♠ 9-6-5-3 ♡ K-Q-4 ◇ A-8-7 ♣ A-10-9 Two notrump
5. ♠ K-8-7-5-4 ♡ A-Q ◇ 8-3 ♣ A-Q-7-3 Two clubs

TRIPLE RAISE OF A MAJOR

A raise of partner's major suit to 4, by an unpassed hand, is a preëmptive bid. It shows: **x-x-x-x-x** (5 cards or more) in trumps

8 to **12** points including a singleton or void not more than 9 pts. in high cards usually, 5-5-2-1 or 6-5-1-1 distribution

If the responder passed originally, he should have 11 to 13 points. This is a strong response.

Examples, partner having bid one heart:
1. ♠ 6 ♡ Q-8-7-5-2 ◇ A-7-6-5-3 ♣ 8-2 Four hearts
2. ♠ 6-5 ♡ 9-7-6-5-3-2 ◇ K-J-6-4-3 ♣ — Four hearts

15

RAISES OF PARTNER'S MINOR SUIT

Situation: Partner has made an opening bid of one diamond or one club; the next player has passed. A raise should seldom be given if any other proper response (except one notrump) is available. A minor suit should seldom be raised without at least 4 trumps, Q-x-x-x or J-10-x-x or better; 3-card support should be K-J-x .

SINGLE RAISE OF A MINOR

A raise of partner's minor suit to two is not forcing. It denies a *biddable* major suit, with which a one-over-one response would be made. The raise requires:

4 trumps, usually Q-x-x-x or better
or 3 trumps, K-J-x or better

6 to **10** points (no more)

Examples, partner having bid one diamond:
1. ♠ 6 ♡ 7-5-3 ◇ Q-8-7-3 ♣ K-8-6-5-2 Two diamonds
2. ♠ 6 ♡ 7-5-3 ◇ K-J-4 ♣ A-8-6-5-3-2 Two diamonds
3. ♠ Q-10-6-5 ♡ 7 ◇ K-8-7-3 ♣ 9-7-5-4 One spade
4. ♠ 6 ♡ 7-5-3 ◇ Q-10-5 ♣ A-8-6-5-3-2 One notrump

DOUBLE RAISE OF A MINOR

A jump raise of partner's minor suit to three is *forcing to game,** unless the responder has previously passed. Requirements are:

Five trumps or four very strong trumps

13 to **16** points (no more)

Examples, partner having bid one diamond:
1. ♠ 6-3 ♡ K-6 ◇ K-Q-7-4-3 ♣ K-6-3-2 Three diamonds
2. ♠ 6-2 ♡ J-5 ◇ K-Q-J-8 ♣ K-J-6-3-2 Three diamonds
3. ♠ K-6-3-2 ♡ K-6 ◇ K-Q-7-4-3 ♣ 6-3 One spade

*Many experts use the double raise of a minor as invitational but not forcing and reduce the requirements to 10-12 points. Some experts use it as a preëmptive bid and the single raise as a strong bid—see page 91.

TRIPLE RAISE OF A MINOR

A raise of partner's minor suit to four is a preëmptive bid, made only on a two-suited hand (usually 6-5-1-1, 6-5-2-0 or 5-5-3-0) when both of the long suits are minor. This bid passes the three-notrump level and should never be made with more than 6 points in high cards. The bid is not forcing or encouraging and the opener should pass it unless he had a strong bid, or strength in both minor suits.

Examples, partner having bid one club:
1. ♠ 7 ♡ 2 ◇ Q-8-6-5-3 ♣ K-8-6-5-3-2 Four clubs
2. ♠ 7 ♡ 5-2 ◇ 10-9-8-7-3 ♣ A-Q-8-6-4 Four clubs

SUIT TAKEOUTS

Situation: Partner has made an opening suit-bid of one; the next player has passed.

Usually a non-jump suit takeout—one in a suit higher-ranking than partner's suit, or two in a suit lower-ranking than partner's suit—is preferred to any other response.

A suit takeout is *forcing for one round* unless the responder has previously passed, and usually the opener rebids over a suit takeout even if the responder passed originally.

THE ONE-OVER-ONE

A takeout in a higher-ranking suit than partner's at the one-level may range from a very weak hand—weaker than a one-notrump response—to a very strong hand. It requires:

Any 7-card or longer major suit

3 high-card points, 6-card major suit

4 high-card points, 5-card major suit

5 high-card points, any biddable suit

The strength of the hand may range upwards to 20 points. However, with 18 points or more consider a forcing takeout (page 20); with 13 points consider a jump notrump response (page 13) or a double raise in a major suit (page 15).

Examples, partner having bid one club:
1. ♠ K-3 ♡ 8-6-5-2 ◇ K-8-5-3 ♣ 7-5-4 One diamond
2. ♠ Q-J-6-5-3-2 ♡ 9-6 ◇ 7-4-3 ♣ 5-4 One spade
3. ♠ A-K-10-5-2 ♡ A-Q-6 ◇ Q-7 ♣ 8-6-2 One spade
4. ♠ K-3 ♡ K-Q-J-9-7-6-3 ◇ 7-2 ♣ K-5 One heart
5. ♠ 8-7-5-3-2 ♡ J-6-3 ◇ 7-4 ♣ A-6-3 One spade

THE TWO-OVER-ONE

A suit takeout in a lower-ranking suit increases the bidding level and therefore requires a stronger hand than the one-over-one response. The minimums are:

**10 points, 7-card or longer major suit
(or a two-suiter including a 6-card suit)**

11 points, 6-card suit (or any biddable suit with strong support for partner's suit)

12 points or more, any biddable suit

Examples, partner having bid one spade:
1. ♠ 8-5 ♡ A-6-5 ◇ K-J-10-6-5-4 ♣ 9-3 Two diamonds
2. ♠ K-6 ♡ 8-6-3 ◇ K-Q-4-3-2 ♣ A-5-4 Two diamonds
3. ♠ 8-6-4-3 ♡ 9 ◇ A-6-3 ♣ K-Q-8-5-2 Two clubs
4. ♠ 6 ♡ A-7-4-3 ◇ Q-8-5-2 ♣ A-Q-9-5 Two clubs
5. ♠ Q-5 ♡ 9-4-3 ◇ A-K-6-5-4 ♣ 10-6-2 One notrump

OPTIONAL RESPONSES TO ONE-BIDS
The Forcing One-Notrump Response

Especially among players who do not open 4-card major suits, a response of one notrump to a *major-suit* bid of one is often used as a one-round forcing bid.

The one-notrump response is forcing only if the opening bidder has not passed originally and if there has been no overcall.

SOUTH	WEST	NORTH	EAST	SOUTH	WEST	NORTH	EAST
1 ♡	Pass	1 N T *Forcing*		1 ◇	Pass	1 N T *Not forcing*	

SOUTH	WEST	NORTH	EAST	SOUTH	WEST	NORTH	EAST
Pass	Pass	1 ♠	Pass	1 ♡	1 ♠	1 N T *Not forcing*	
1 N T *Not forcing*							

Although forcing, the one-notrump response never shows a strong hand. It is used to permit the responder to deny strength in high cards but still assure himself a later chance to show his distribution.

Partner opens 1 ♠, right-hand opponent passes.

1. ♠ 6-3   ♡ K-7-2   ◇ 8-7   ♣ Q-J-9-6-5-3
Respond 1 N T, at second turn bid clubs, showing a long club suit in a weak hand.

2. ♠ 8-7-5-2   ♡ 7-5   ◇ Q-6   ♣ Q-8-6-5-4
Respond 1 N T, at second turn raise spades, showing weak raise.

3. ♠ 8-6   ♡ J-7-5   ◇ Q-6-3   ♣ A-Q-10-5-2
Respond 1 N T, at second turn bid 2 N T, showing good hand but less than enough to bid 2 ♣ over 1 ♠.

The forcing one-notrump response never replaces a one-over-one response, whether the responding hand is strong or weak.

Partner bids 1 ♡, right-hand opponent passes.

1. ♠ Q-J-8-5-3   ♡ 7-6   ◇ K-6-2   ♣ 8-4-3   Bid one spade
2. ♠ K-J-8-4   ♡ 8-6-5-3   ◇ Q-7-6   ♣ 7-4   Bid one spade
3. ♠ J-9-8-7-5-3-2   ♡ 6   ◇ A-8-5   ♣ 7-4   Bid one spade

The forcing one-notrump response is used to distinguish between strong and weak single raises.

Partner opens 1 ♠, right-hand opponent passes.

1. ♠ J-6-5-3   ♡ Q-6-3   ◇ 10-7-6   ♣ K-8-5
Respond 1 N T, raise spades later.

2. ♠ J-6-5-3   ♡ Q-6   ◇ A-J-7-5-2   ♣ 7-3
Bid 2 ♠ as first response.

A one-notrump response to a minor-suit bid is never forcing, but it *may* be stronger than the one-notrump response to a major suit, showing 6 to 10 high-card points and denying any suit in which a one-over-one response could be made.

Partner bids 1 ◇, right-hand opponent passes.

1. ♠ A-Q-4   ♡ K-6   ◇ J-8-5   ♣ 10-8-6-3-2   One notrump
2. ♠ J-7   ♡ J-6-2   ◇ 7-5-4   ♣ A-K-7-3-2   One notrump
3. ♠ 8-6   ♡ Q-7-6-5   ◇ 8-6-2   ♣ A-8-6-4   One heart
4. ♠ 6-3-2   ♡ K-7-6   ◇ 4   ♣ Q-J-9-7-6-3   Pass

OPTIONAL RESPONSES TO ONE-BIDS

Limited Jump Raise in Majors

A raise of an opening 1 ♡ to 3 ♡, or of 1 ♠ to 3 ♠, shows 4-card trump support and 10 to 12 high-card points, but is not forcing.

South opens 1 ♠, North responds 3 ♠. North holds:
♠ Q-10-6-3   ♡ A-7   ◇ K-Q-8-6   ♣ 8-5-4
South may pass a minimum.

Three-Notrump Forcing Response

Players using the limited jump raise in a major often use three notrump as a game-forcing response showing strong, 4-card or longer trump support and 13 to 15 high-card points.

South opens 1 ♠, North responds 3 N T. North holds:
♠ K-J-5-4-2   ♡ 6   ◇ A-K-7-3   ♣ Q-6-3
South must rebid and may bid 4 ♠ on any biddable suit.

Inverted Minor Raises

In this popular method, a jump raise of 1 ♣ to 3 ♣ or 1 ◇ to 3 ◇ is preëmptive, showing length in trumps but a weak hand in high cards (usually 8 pts. or less in high cards); a single raise, from 1 ♣ to 2 ♣ or from 1 ◇ to 2 ◇, shows 12 pts. or more and perhaps only strong 3-card trump support.

1.	SOUTH	WEST	NORTH	EAST	*North holds:*
	1 ◇	Pass	3 ◇		

1. ♠ 8
   ♡ Q-8-4
   ◇ K-J-8-6-2
   ♣ J-7-5-4

2. ♠ Q-6
   ♡ A-10-8
   ◇ K-9-4-3
   ♣ K-8-6-2

2.	SOUTH	WEST	NORTH	EAST
	1 ◇	Pass	2 ◇	

Preëmptive Raise in Competition

This convention makes any single raise over an opponent's overcall weak (8 pts. or less in high cards) but adequate trump support is required.

SOUTH WEST NORTH EAST   *North holds:* ♠ 6-3-2
1 ♡   2 ◇   2 ♡   ♡ J-8-5-3
                                          ◇ 6
                                          ♣ Q-J-7-5-2

Drury Convention

This is a bidding device introduced by Alan Drury for use over partner's third- or fourth-hand opening bid, to determine the soundness of the bid. A two-club response to the opening bid asks the opener to clarify his hand. If opener has made a substandard bid he rebids two diamonds; any other rebid verifies a sound opening. The two-club response is artificial (not promising club strength) and is forcing.

SOUTH WEST NORTH EAST   *North holds:* ♠ Q-J-10-8-2
Pass   Pass 1 ♠   Pass   ♡ A-J-3
2 ♣   Pass 2 ◇   ◇ 9-5
                                          ♣ K-9-4

POINT-COUNT VALUATION

BIDDABLE SUITS

OPENING ONE-BIDS

CHOICE OF SUITS

FORCING BIDS

RESPONSES TO SUIT-BIDS

OPENER'S REBIDS

RESPONDER'S REBIDS

NOTRUMP BIDDING

OPENING 3, 4, 5 BIDS

FORCING TWO-BIDS

OVERCALLS

TAKEOUT DOUBLE

PENALTY DOUBLES

PART-SCORE

DUPLICATE

SLAM BIDS

4-5 NOTRUMP SLAM BIDS

BIDDING CONVENTIONS

PERCENTAGE TABLES

BIDDING SYSTEMS

OPENING LEADS

SIGNALS IN PLAY

COVERING HONORS

FINESSES

SAFETY PLAYS

END-PLAYS SQUEEZE

BRIDGE LAWS

GLOSSARY

JUMP SUIT TAKEOUTS

Situation: Partner has made an opening suit-bid of one; the next player has passed.

A jump response of *exactly one trick* more than necessary (as two spades over partner's one diamond, or three clubs over partner's one heart) is forcing: if the responder has not previously passed, it shows a powerful hand in high cards and is forcing to game; if the responder has previously passed, it shows a maximum pass and is forcing for at least one round.

A jump of *more than one trick* in a new suit is a preëmptive bid. It shows a hand whose strength is centered in one long suit, with little or no defensive values.

THE FORCING TAKEOUT

A single-jump takeout, called also a *jump shift,* when the responder has not previously passed, requires:

18 points with a solid suit or strong support for partner's suit

20 points with a fit in partner's suit

21 points or more with any distribution

Examples, partner having bid one heart:
1. ♠ A-Q-5-3 ♡ 6-2 ◇ A-K-5 ♣ A-K-4-2 Two spades
2. ♠ 3 ♡ Q-10-5-4 ◇ A-K-5 ♣ A-K-10-5-3 Three clubs
3. ♠ A-5 ♡ 2 ◇ A-K-Q-J-8-5-3 ♣ K-8-2 Three diamonds
4. ♠ A-K-Q-7-2 ♡ 3-2 ◇ A-K-7-6-3 ♣ 5 Two spades

Having passed originally, a player should make a forcing takeout with 11 to 13 points and a strong two-suiter or strong support for partner's suit.

Partner, third or fourth hand, having bid one diamond.
1. ♠ K-10-9-8-6-3 ♡ K-Q-J-7-2 ◇ 8-2 ♣ — Two spades
2. ♠ A-Q-8 ♡ 6-5 ◇ Q-8-7-3-2 ♣ A-7-4 Three clubs

THE DOUBLE JUMP TO THREE

A double jump to three of a suit, as 3 ♠ over 1 ◇ or 3 ◇ over 1 ♣, shows a long suit in a weak hand and (a) denies support for partner's suit; (b) denies length in an outside major suit; (c) denies high-card strength, showing

not more than 6 points in high cards

The opener should pass unless his hand is very strong (17 or more points).

Examples, partner having bid one diamond:
1. ♠ Q-J-9-8-6-5-3 ♡ 7-3 ◇ 6-4 ♣ 8-7 Three spades
2. ♣ 6-2 ♡ A-Q-10-9-7-6 ◇ 5 ♣ 7-5-4-2 Three hearts

POINT-COUNT
VALUATION

BIDDABLE
SUITS

OPENING
ONE-BIDS

CHOICE
OF SUITS

FORCING BIDS

RESPONSES
TO SUIT-BIDS

OPENER'S
REBIDS

RESPONDER'S
REBIDS

NOTRUMP
BIDDING

OPENING
3, 4, 5 BIDS

FORCING
TWO-BIDS

OVERCALLS

TAKEOUT
DOUBLE

PENALTY
DOUBLES

PART-SCORE

DUPLICATE

SLAM BIDS

4-5 NOTRUMP
SLAM BIDS

BIDDING
CONVENTIONS

PERCENTAGE
TABLES

BIDDING
SYSTEMS

OPENING
LEADS

SIGNALS
IN PLAY

COVERING
HONORS

FINESSES

SAFETY PLAYS

END-PLAYS
SQUEEZE

BRIDGE LAWS

GLOSSARY

JUMP SUIT TAKEOUTS (Cont'd)
THE JUMP TO FOUR

A jump to four of a major suit over partner's opening bid in another suit shows a strong suit of 7 or 8 cards, little or no defensive strength outside the trump suit, little or no hope of a slam, and

not more than 8 points in high cards

The opener should pass unless, with at least an honor in the responder's suit and three aces, or two aces and a singleton or void, he can try for a slam.

A jump to four in a minor suit should be avoided, except with a freak hand including an 8- or 9-card suit.

Examples, partner having bid one diamond:
1. ♠ A-Q-J-10-7-5-4-2 ♡ 7 ◇ 6 ♣ 6-4-2 Four spades
2. ♠ 6 ♡ 3 ◇ 7-3 ♣ K-Q-9-8-7-5-4-3-2 Four clubs

FREE RESPONSES

Situation: Partner's opening suit-bid of one has been overcalled by your right-hand opponent. You need not bid a weak hand to keep the bidding open. Any response you make shows strength.

SOUTH	WEST	NORTH	EAST		SOUTH	WEST	NORTH	EAST
1 ◇	Pass				1 ◇	1 ♡		

(If North passes, East may pass and South will not get another chance.)

(South will get another chance even if North passes. Any response by North is a free bid.)

REQUIREMENTS FOR FREE RESPONSES

SINGLE RAISE

8 to 11 points with adequate trump support. *Not forcing.* With 10 or 11 pts. raise with as little as x-x-x (three small cards) in partner's major suit, but prefer any available one-over-one or two-over-one response (see below).

DOUBLE RAISE (Non-jump)

9 to 12 points with 4-card trump support. *Not forcing.* With 11 or 12 points, trump support for a major suit may be reduced to three cards, K-x-x or better, if no suit response is available. Avoid a double raise in a minor without 5-card or strong 4-card trump support.

Continued on next page.

21

Situation: Partner's opening suit-bid of one has been overcalled by your right-hand opponent. You need not bid a weak hand to keep the bidding open. Any response you make shows strength.

REQUIREMENTS FOR FREE RESPONSES

ONE NOTRUMP	**10 to 12 points** in high cards with at least one stopper (K-x-x or Q-J-x or better) in the opponent's suit. *Not forcing.*
TWO NOTRUMP (Non-jump)	**13 to 15 points** in high cards with a double stopper (K-J-x or better) in the opponent's suit. *Forcing for one round.* About the same hand as required for a jump response of two notrump—see p. 13.
ONE-OVER-ONE	**9 points** or more with a 4- or 5-card suit. *Forcing for one round.*
TWO-OVER-ONE (Non-jump)	**11 points** or more with a 5-card or longer suit (about the same hand as if there had been no overcall). BUT: If your suit is higher-ranking than partner's, or if you must bid three to show it, you need at least **12 pts.** with a strong trump suit.

A jump response should be made, disregarding the opposing overcall, when the hands meets the requirements. A penalty double should always be considered (page 56).

When Partner Bid One Notrump

When partner's opening one-notrump bid is overcalled, a non-jump suit-bid by the responder is *not forcing* and *denies enough strength to raise in notrump or double.*

SOUTH	WEST	NORTH	EAST	SOUTH	WEST	NORTH	EAST
1 N T	2 ♠	3 ♣	Pass	1 N T	2 ◇	3 ♡	Pass
(North denies strength.)				(North's bid is forcing.)			

With 10 or more points raise the notrump (even without a stopper in the opponent's suit); or double; or make a jump response in a suit.

REBIDS BY THE OPENER
Over a Suit Takeout

Situation: You have opened with a suit-bid of one. Partner has made a suit takeout (a one-over-one or a non-jump two-over-one response). The next player has passed.

Partner's response is *forcing for one round,* EXCEPT you may pass (a) if partner passed originally; or (b) if your side has a part-score and partner's bid is enough for game. Even then you should usually rebid if you have anything more than a minimum opening bid or if you cannot support partner's suit.

With 20 or more points, see page 27.

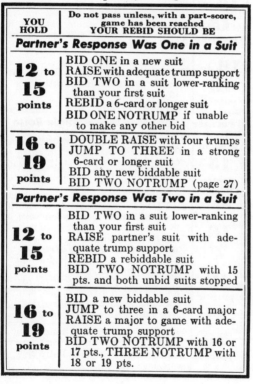

YOU HOLD	Do not pass unless, with a part-score, game has been reached. YOUR REBID SHOULD BE
Partner's Response Was One in a Suit	
12 to 15 points	BID ONE in a new suit RAISE with adequate trump support BID TWO in a suit lower-ranking than your first suit REBID a 6-card or longer suit BID ONE NOTRUMP if unable to make any other bid
16 to 19 points	DOUBLE RAISE with four trumps JUMP TO THREE in a strong 6-card or longer suit BID any new biddable suit BID TWO NOTRUMP (page 27)
Partner's Response Was Two in a Suit	
12 to 15 points	BID TWO in a suit lower-ranking than your first suit RAISE partner's suit with adequate trump support REBID a rebiddable suit BID TWO NOTRUMP with 15 pts. and both unbid suits stopped
16 to 19 points	BID a new biddable suit JUMP to three in a 6-card major RAISE a major to game with adequate trump support BID TWO NOTRUMP with 16 or 17 pts., THREE NOTRUMP with 18 or 19 pts.

REBIDS BY THE OPENER (Cont'd)

Situation: You have opened with a suit-bid of one. Partner has responded one notrump, or has raised your suit to two. Both opponents have passed.

The response is not forcing. *You may pass,* but rebid if you have the required strength, as shown below. With 20 or more points, see page 27.

YOU HOLD	YOUR REBID SHOULD BE
Partner's Response Was One Notrump	
12 to 15 points	BID a new biddable suit (lower-ranking than your first suit) with unbalanced distribution REBID a 6-card suit PASS with less
16 to 19 points	BID a new biddable suit REBID a rebiddable suit RAISE to two notrump with 18 or 19 pts. Otherwise, PASS
Partner's Response Was a Single Raise	
12 to 15 points	PASS—but there are exceptions: Bid *three* in a 6-card major suit with 14 to 15 pts. Bid three or even four in a 5-card or longer major suit with at least 10 cards in two suits.
16 to 19 points	REBID a 5-card or longer major to *three* with 16-17 pts., to four with 18-19 pts. or with highly unbalanced distribution (at least 10 cards in two suits) BID three in a new biddable suit (*forcing for one round*) BID two notrump (*forcing for one round*) with a 4-card major, or if the suit raised was a minor PASS only with 4-4-3-2 and 16 pts.
20 points	DO NOT PASS. Bid four in a 5-card or longer major with balanced distribution; or bid a new suit or notrump.

REBIDS BY THE OPENER (Cont'd)
Over a Jump Forcing Response

Situation: You have opened with a suit-bid of one. Partner has made a jump response—*exactly one trick* more than necessary. The next player has passed.

Partner's response is *forcing to game.* However, a double raise or a two-notrump response may be passed if (with a part-score) it is enough for game. A forcing takeout (also called a jump shift) is forcing for at least one round in any case.

Over a Jump Raise in a Major Suit

Pass only if the contract is enough for game and you cannot make a slam try, or if partner passed originally and you have a minimum opening bid.

Bid three notrump with 4-3-3-3 or 4-4-3-2 distribution.

Bid FOUR in your suit in every other case, unless you can make a slam try.

Any bid in a new suit is a slam try. Try for a slam with 17 or more points (see page 60).

You opened one heart. Partner responded three hearts. Your rebid:
1. ♠ K-6 ♡ A-J-6-2 ◇ K-8-5-4 ♣ Q-J-7   Three notrump
2. ♠ 8-2 ♡ K-8-7-5-4 ◇ A-K-Q-4 ♣ Q-3   Four hearts

Over a Jump Raise in a Minor Suit

Do not pass unless there is clear agreement that the double raise is not forcing (see page 16).

Bid three notrump with balanced distribution.

Show a strong 4-card major (partner's double raise probably denies a biddable major).

Bid four or five in a long suit with unbalanced distribution.

You opened one club. Partner raised to three clubs. Your rebid:
1. ♠ Q-6 ♡ K-J-7-4 ◇ Q-6-3 ♣ A-K-5-3   Three notrump
2. ♠ A-Q-9-6 ♡ 7-3 ◇ J-8-4 ♣ A-K-6-5   Three spades
3. ♠ 9 ♡ 10 ◇ A-K-6-3 ♣ K-J-9-7-6-5-2   Five clubs

Over a Two-Notrump Takeout

Do not pass unless the contract is enough for game, or partner passed originally and you have a minimum.

Bid three in a rebiddable major suit; or in a new biddable suit.

Raise to three notrump with any other hand, unless you can make a slam try (page 60).

You opened one spade. Partner responded two notrump. Your rebid:
♠ K-Q-J-8-3 ♡ A-6-2 ◇ K-8-7 ♣ 9-2   Three spades
♠ K-J-9-4-3 ♡ A-Q-8 ◇ K-8-7 ♣ J-5   Three notrump

Continued on next page

REBIDS BY THE OPENER (Cont'd)
Over a Forcing Takeout
Do not pass.
Rebid a rebiddable suit, or bid notrump, at the lowest level. These rebids show a possible minimum.

Raise with adequate trump support.

Bid a new biddable suit. This rebid is preferred when opener has additional values, but does not guarantee them.

A DOUBLE-JUMP RESPONSE in a suit is a preëmptive bid and may be passed. A jump response of three notrump is strength-showing. It may be passed but opener should make a slam try with 16 or more points.

STRENGTH-SHOWING REBIDS

Situation: You have opened with a suit-bid of one. Partner has made a non-jump response. With 18 or more points consider the following rebids.

A Forcing Rebid is a jump of exactly one trick more than necessary in a new suit. It is the strongest rebid the opener can make and is *forcing to game*. It requires:

19 or more points with a strong two-suiter or strong support for responder's suit

You opened one diamond. Partner responded one heart. Rebid:
1. ♠ 6 ♡ K-J-3 ◇ A-K-7-5-2 ♣ A-K-J-7 Three clubs
2. ♠ A-K-J-7-3 ♡ 6 ◇ A-K-8-7-6-3 ♣ 9 Two spades
3. ♠ — ♡ K-J-5-3 ◇ A-J-8-5-4 ♣ A-K-6-5 Three clubs

A Reverse Bid is a voluntary rebid of *two or more* in a suit higher in rank than the suit you bid first. It is *not forcing* but it shows strength because it may force partner to the three-level to show preference. Requirements are:

18 to 20 points with a 5-card suit (bid first) and a 4-card suit (bid second)

16 or more points with 6-5 distribution

You opened one diamond. Partner responded one spade. Rebid:
1. ♠ 3 ♡ A-K-8-5 ◇ A-K-7-6-2 ♣ K-5-4 Two hearts
2. ♠ 3 ♡ A-J-8-4-3 ◇ A-K-7-6-4-3 ♣ 4 Two hearts

The 6-5 distribution of Hand No. 2 is shown by rebidding the second-bid suit at the next opportunity. A suit rebid at the *one-level* is not strength-showing. A forced reverse bid at the two-level or higher is not necessarily strength-showing.

REBIDS BY THE OPENER (Cont'd)
Strength-Showing Rebids

Situation: You have opened with *one in a suit.* Partner has made a nonjump suit or notrump response. With 4 or more points above a minimum, consider the following rebids. *None is forcing.*

A Jump Rebid of Three in a MAJOR suit in which you opened the bidding requires 19-21 pts., or:

17 points with a strong 7-card suit

18 points with a strong 6-card suit

19 or more points with a very strong 5-card suit

You opened one heart. Partner responded one notrump Rebid:
1. ♠ 6   ♡ K-Q-J-7-6-5-2   ◇ A-6-3   ♣ A-4   Three hearts
2. ♠ A-6   ♡ A-J-10-7-6-3   ◇ 5   ♣ A-Q-7-5   Three hearts
3. ♠ 9   ♡ A-K-Q-J-4   ◇ A-K-Q   ♣ 10-8-5-3   Three hearts

A Jump to Four in a Major, *when partner has not raised the suit,* shows a stronger hand than the jump to three, by about one trick.

You opened one spade. Partner responded one notrump. Rebid:
♠ A-Q-J-10-6-5-3   ♡ 6   ◇ K-Q-9   ♣ A-4   Four spades

This bid should be used only when partner surely understands it and will make a slam try on a hand of moderate strength.

A Jump Rebid of Three in a MINOR suit in which you opened the bidding shows *seven probable quick winners at notrump:* as, a 6-card suit headed by A-K-Q with an outside ace. It invites a three-notrump bid on 7 to 9 points (or more) in three suits.

You opened one diamond. Partner responded one spade. Rebid:
1. ♠ 6-2   ♡ A-8-3   ◇ A-K-Q-8-6-2   ♣ 7-4   Three diamonds
2. ♠ 6   ♡ 8-3   ◇ A-K-Q-8-6-4-2   ♣ K-7-4   Three diamonds

A Jump to Two Notrump as a rebid shows 18 to 20 points; balanced distribution, and every suit stopped. It may conceal a long, strong suit, or support for partner's suit.

You opened one heart. Partner responded one spade. Rebid:
1. ♠ J-5   ♡ K-Q-6-5-3   ◇ A-K-6   ♣ A-Q-10   Two notrump
2. ♠ A-J-3   ♡ A-J-8-4   ◇ K-Q-6-3   ♣ A-8   Two notrump

A Jump to Three Notrump as a rebid shows a stronger hand than the jump to two, by about one trick.

You opened one club. Partner responded one diamond. Rebid:
♠ A-K-6   ♡ K-J-7   ◇ Q-3   ♣ A-K-Q-7-5   Three notrump

This bid invites a slam try if partner has 10 points or more, but it should be used sparingly because partner will usually pass.

FREE REBIDS BY THE OPENER

Situation: You opened with a suit-bid of one. It is your turn again, but the last bid was an opponent's overcall. For example:

SOUTH	WEST	NORTH	EAST	SOUTH	WEST	NORTH	EAST
1 ◇	Pass	1 ♡	1 ♠	1 ◇	Pass	Pass	1 ♡

If South bids, it is a free bid. | If South bids, it is a free bid.

You may pass, but with added values rebid as indicated below. A strength-showing rebid (page 27) should usually be made regardless of the opening overcall, and a penalty double should be considered (page 56). When partner has passed your opening bid he cannot be relied upon for any support and any rebid should comply with the Rule of 2 & 3 (page 41).

YOU HOLD	YOUR REBID SHOULD BE
When Partner Has Responded	
14 points or less	RAISE once with 4 trumps REBID a strong 6-card suit PASS with less
15 to **17** points	BID ONE in a new suit BID TWO in a 6-card suit or in a new 5-card suit RAISE with adequate trump support BID ONE NOTRUMP with a stopper in the opponent's suit PASS with less
18 points or more	REBID according to page 25, but bid notrump only with the opponents' suit stopped
When Partner Did Not Respond	
16 points or less	Usually, PASS BID TWO with a strong rebiddable suit or a 5-5 two-suiter
17 to **20** points	DOUBLE (takeout double) with support for the unbid suits; or REBID or pass as shown above

28

REBIDS BY THE RESPONDER

Situation: You made a non-jump response to partner's opening suit-bid of one. Partner made a non-jump rebid. The opponents have not bid.

SOUTH	WEST	NORTH	EAST	SOUTH	WEST	NORTH	EAST
1 ◊	Pass	1 ♠	Pass	1 ◊	Pass	1 ♡	Pass
2 ♣	Pass			1 ♠	Pass		

SOUTH	WEST	NORTH	EAST	SOUTH	WEST	NORTH	EAST
1 ◊	Pass	1 ♠	Pass	1 ◊	Pass	1 ♠	Pass
1 N T	Pass			2 ♣			

Partner's rebid is not forcing. *You may pass.* Any rebid you make in a new suit is forcing for one round (unless it is enough for game).

YOU HOLD	YOUR REBID SHOULD BE
6 points or less	PASS, or show preference Over a one-notrump rebid, bid a second 5-card suit (*not forcing*)
7 to **9** pts.	REBID a 6-card suit or a new 5-card suit ONE NOTRUMP, over a one-bid PASS or show preference with less
10 or **11** points	BID TWO in a suit or notrump RAISE partner's suit with adequate trump support RAISE a notrump rebid once PASS if your first response showed your full strength
12 points or more	BID THREE in a suit or notrump RAISE partner's suit twice with adequate trump support Do not pass

If the Opener's Rebid Was a Raise

6 points or less	Usually, PASS. But rebid a 6-card or longer major with unbalanced distribution.
7 to **9** points	Usually, PASS. But rebid if partner raised one notrump to two, or a suit to three
10 points or more	REBID a rebiddable major suit BID a new biddable suit SHOW SUPPORT for partner's suit BID TWO NOTRUMP (or 3 NT, if partner raised 1 NT to two).

REBIDS BY THE RESPONDER (Cont'd)

Situation: You made a non-jump response to partner's opening suit-bid of one. Partner has made a jump rebid—exactly one trick more than necessary. The opponents have not bid.

South	West	North	East
1 ◊	Pass	1 ♠	Pass
2 N T	Pass		

South	West	North	East
1 ◊	Pass	1 ♠	Pass
3 ♠	Pass		

South	West	North	East
1 ♡	Pass	1 N T	Pass
3 ♡	Pass		

South	West	North	East
1 ◊	Pass	1 ♠	Pass
2 ♡	(Reverse bid—see p. 26)		

Partner's rebid is not forcing, but you should not pass unless you had a minimum for the first response or there is danger of a misfit. Any rebid you make, short of game, is *forcing to game.*

YOU HOLD	YOUR REBID SHOULD BE
Over a Jump Rebid	
5 pts. or less in high cards	PASS two notrump or a reverse bid. Rebid own major with 6-card or longer suit; raise a major with x-x-x or 10-x and a singleton.
6 to **8** points in high cards	RAISE or show preference (4-card support is needed to raise a reverse bid) REBID a raised 5-card major BID THREE NOTRUMP *Do not pass*
9 points or more	BID GAME in a major suit or no-trump (but do not raise a reverse bid without 4-card support) TRY FOR A SLAM if able (page 60); a bid in a new suit is usually a slam try

Over Other Jump Rebids

A forcing rebid (jump shift) by the opener (page 26) is forcing to game and may not be passed. The responder should rebid as the opener rebids over a forcing takeout (page 25).

If the opener bids four of a major over a single raise, or raises a 1 N T response to 3 N T, the responder MUST ALWAYS PASS.

If the opener makes a double-jump rebid of 3 N T or four of a major, he shows a stronger hand than by a single jump. Responder may pass but should make a slam try with 12 points or more.

REBIDS BY THE RESPONDER (Cont'd)
How to Show Preference
When your partner has bid two suits, do not pass the second if you have better support for the first.

1. *Prefer the suit in which you are longer.* (With ♠ A-Q and ♡ 4-3-2, prefer hearts.)
2. With equal length in his suits, usually prefer the one he bid first.

SOUTH	NORTH	North should bid two spades with:
1 ♠	1 N T	♠ 7-6-3 ♡ A-8-4-2 ◇ K-6-4 ♣ 8-7-6
2 ◇		North should pass with:
		♠ A-5 ♡ Q-7-6-3 ◇ 6-3-2 ♣ 10-7-6-2

If strong enough to raise: Raise one trick in the second-bid suit, or jump one trick in the first-bid suit. If partner's second-bid suit is higher-ranking than his first suit, do not raise it without four trumps, unless he rebids it.

Strength-Showing Rebids
Situation: Partner opened with a suit-bid of one. You responded with a nonjump suit-bid. Partner has made a minimum rebid. With 13 or more points, consider the following rebids.

A Forcing Rebid—a bid of exactly one trick more than necessary in a new suit—is forcing to game. It requires:

13 or more points if partner's rebid was one notrump			**16** or more points if a nonjump rebid would be forcing		
SOUTH	NORTH	*North has:*	SOUTH	NORTH	*North has:*
1 ◇	1 ♠	♠ K-J-7-5-3	1 ◇	1 ♠	♠ A-Q-7-5-3
1 N T	3 ♡	♡ A-Q-J-4-2	2 ◇	3 ♡	♡ A-K-9-4-2
	(Forcing to game)	◇ 10-6		*(Suggests a slam)*	◇ 10-6
		♣ 5			♣ 5

This is the only rebid by responder that is forcing even if game has been reached, with a part-score. The opener should rebid as he would over an immediate forcing takeout—see page 22.

A Jump Rebid in the Same Suit that the responder bid first. This is *not* a forcing bid, but it is rarely passed. Requirements are:

12 or 13 points with a strong 5-card or longer suit.

SOUTH	NORTH	*North has:*	SOUTH	NORTH	*North has:*
1 ◇	1 ♡	♠ A-2	1 ◇	1 ♠	♠ K-Q-10--5-3o
1 ♠	3 ♡	♡ A-Q-J-8-7	1 N T	3 ♠	♡ A-5-4
(Not forcing)		◇ 7-4-3	*(Not forcing)*		◇ J-6
		♣ 8-5-3			♣ 7-5

The opener should pass only if he has a minimum hand and cannot support the responder's suit or bid notrump.

REBIDS BY THE RESPONDER (Cont'd)
Strength-Showing Rebids

Situation: You have opened with *one in a suit.* Partner has made a nonjump suit or notrump response. With 4 or more points above a minimum, consider the following rebids. *None is forcing.*

A Jump to Two Notrump. This can occur only when the opener made a one-over-one rebid. The 2 N T rebid is *not* forcing but is rarely passed. It requires:

11 or 12 points (no more) in a 4-3-3-3 or 4-4-3-2 hand

The opener will pass only with a minimum including two wholly unguarded suits.

SOUTH	NORTH	North may hold:	South will pass:
1 ♥	1 ♥	♠ 7-5-4	♠ A-K-8-2
1 ♣	2 N T	♡ K-10-7-3	♡ 6-4
		◇ A-K-8	◇ 7-5-4
		♣ J-6-4	♣ A-Q-7-3

A Jump to Three Notrump shows a stronger hand than the jump to two notrump but it is *not forcing* and it is a limited bid, not a slam try. It requires:

13 to 16 points (no more) with balanced distribution

In the bidding example above, North would rebid 3 N T on:
♠ Q-3   ♡ A-J-8-7-2   ◇ A-K-8   ♣ 9-6-4

A Jump Raise in any suit bid by opener is a strength-showing rebid by responder and by many players is treated as forcing. Examples are:

1. SOUTH NORTH	2. SOUTH NORTH	3. SOUTH NORTH
1 ♥ 1 ♠	1 ◇ 1 ♥	1 ♣ 1 ♠
2 ♥ 3 ♥	1 ♠ 3 ♠	1 N T 3 ♣

In the absence of clear agreement to the contrary, the opener should treat North's jump as forcing. However, North's raise shows limited strength—

about 13 supporting points with adequate trump support
(4-card support needed in cases 2 & 3)

In the bidding sequences above, North may hold:
1. ♠ A-K-8-5-2   ♡ Q-9-3   ◇ 7-2   ♣ Q-6-5   Three hearts
2. ♠ J-9-7-3   ♡ A-J-7-4   ◇ 6   ♣ A-10-8-3   Three spades
3. ♠ K-J-5-4   ♡ Q-6   ◇ 7-4-3   ♣ A-Q-6-5   Three clubs

A Reverse Rebid by the responder—a rebid in a new suit higher-ranking than the suit responder bid first—is forcing and by many players is treated as *forcing to game.* It may show anywhere from 13 to 18 points with two suits, of which the second-bid suit is probably a 4-card suit.

SOUTH	NORTH	North may hold:
1 ♣	1 ◇	♠ A-Q-10-6 ♡ 8 ◇ A-K-9-6-3 ♣ 7-5-2
2 ♣	2 ♠	or ♠ K-9-7-6-3 ♡ 8 ◇ A-Q-J-8-5-3 ♣ 6

POINT-COUNT
VALUATION

BIDDABLE
SUITS

OPENING
ONE-BIDS

CHOICE
OF SUITS

FORCING BIDS

RESPONSES
TO SUIT-BIDS

OPENER'S
REBIDS

RESPONDER'S
REBIDS

NOTRUMP
BIDDING

OPENING
3, 4, 5 BIDS

FORCING
TWO-BIDS

OVERCALLS

TAKEOUT
DOUBLE

PENALTY
DOUBLES

PART-SCORE

DUPLICATE

SLAM BIDS

4-5 NOTRUMP
SLAM BIDS

BIDDING
CONVENTIONS

PERCENTAGE
TABLES

BIDDING
SYSTEMS

OPENING
LEADS

SIGNALS
IN PLAY

COVERING
HONORS

FINESSES

SAFETY PLAYS

END-PLAYS
SQUEEZE

BRIDGE LAWS

GLOSSARY

OPENING NOTRUMP BIDS

Any opening notrump bid should show a hand of balanced distribution: 4-3-3-3 (ideal); 4-4-3-2 (almost as good); 5-3-3-2 (when the long suit is a minor).

A notrump bid should not have a range of more than 3 points, such as 16 to 18 points (called "the strong notrump"). Many players reduce this requirement to 15-17 points and some use "the weak notrump" of 12 to 14 points, especially when not vulnerable, but the following requirements are generally accepted.

Open with One Notrump

in any position, vulnerable or not vulnerable, with:

16 to 18 points (no more, no less);
balanced distribution;
high cards in at least three suits,
and preferably in all four.

One notrump may be bid with three or four small cards in the weakest suit. A doubleton in the hand must be Q-x or better.

One notrump may be bid on **15 points** if the hand contains seven or more honor cards (10-spot or higher).

A hand with **19 to 21 points** should be opened with a suit-bid of one. A jump in notrump may be made as a rebid.

Examples of proper opening one-notrump bids:

1.	♠ A-Q-6	♡ A-J-8-4	♢ K-Q-6	♣ 10-7-5	One notrump
2.	♠ Q-10-6-5	♡ A-J	♢ A-Q-7	♣ A-8-5-3	One notrump
3.	♠ K-J-3	♡ A-10-5	♢ Q-J-10-5	♣ A-7-2	One notrump
4.	♠ K-6	♡ Q-J-8	♢ A-K-Q-6-4	♣ Q-6-3	One notrump

Rarely, with a 6-3-2-2 or 5-4-2-2 hand (long suits in minors):

5.	♠ Q-8-4	♡ K-7	♢ A-Q-J-9-8-3	♣ A-10	One notrump
6.	♠ K-3	♡ K-5	♢ A-Q-7-6	♣ A-Q-8-5-4	One notrump

Never with more or less than the requirements:

7.	♠ A-6-3	♡ A-8-4	♢ A-7-2	♣ K-8-6-2	One club
8.	♠ A-K-6	♡ K-6-3	♢ A-J-5-2	♣ A-7-4	One diamond

Open with Two Notrump

(not forcing, but inviting a weak response) with:

22 to 24 points, balanced distribution, no suit weaker than K-x or Q-10-x.

With a solid 5-card minor suit 20 points are enough.

Open with two notrump, any position, holding:

1.	♠ Q-J-6-5	♡ A-K-3	♢ K-Q-J	♣ A-Q-7	Two notrump
2.	♠ K-J-3	♡ A-Q-7	♢ A-K-3	♣ A-Q-3-2	Two notrump
3.	♠ A-6-3	♡ Q-10-5	♢ A-K-Q-J-5	♣ A-8	Two notrump

Continued on next page

33

OPENING NOTRUMP BIDS (Cont'd)

Open with Three Notrump

(not forcing, but a slam try) with

25 to **27** points, always 4-3-3-3 distribution, no suit weaker than A-x or Q-J-x.

This opening bid should be avoided (usually in favor of a forcing two-bid) with a partner who, not appreciating its strength, will not make a slam try on a weak-looking hand.

Open with three notrump, any position, holding:
1. ♠ A-Q-6 ♡ A-K-7-2 ♢ K-Q-J ♣ A-Q-2   Three notrump
2. ♠ A-K-5 ♡ A-K-8 ♢ A-Q-J ♣ K-Q-J-2   Three notrump

Responses to Two Notrump

STAYMAN response if able (page 37)
RAISE (with no long suit) to
    3 N T with **4** to **8** points
    4 N T with **9** points
    5 N T with **10** or **11** points
    6 N T with **12** to **14** points
    7 N T with **15** points or more

ANY SUIT TAKEOUT is forcing to game, showing a 6-card suit or a two-suiter with 4 or more points.
PASS with fewer than 4 points and no long suit.

Partner opened two notrump. Holding:
♠ Q-7-3 ♡ 9-6-5 ♢ Q-10-6-5 ♣ 7-4-2   Three notrump
♠ J-5-4 ♡ 7-6 ♢ Q-8-6-5 ♣ 10-7-6-2   Pass

Responses to Three Notrump

Any response to an opening three-notrump bid is a slam try—see page 60.
RAISE to 4 N T with **7** points, to 6 N T with **8** to **11** points, to 7 N T with **12** points.
BID FOUR in a 5-card or longer suit with **6** points.
PASS with less.

Partner opened three notrump. Holding:
♠ K-8-7-6-3 ♡ K-7-2 ♢ 7 ♣ 8-6-5-2   Bid 4 ♠ (slam try)
♠ 8-7 ♡ Q-6-3 ♢ Q-9-7-4 ♣ K-7-3-2   Bid 4 N T (slam try)

Sign-off Bids

Especially when the Stayman Convention is not used, a suit takeout of one notrump followed by a rebid in the same suit shows a weak hand not suitable for notrump play. The responder warns that game is out of the question and the opener should pass. Some sign off with weak 5-5 two-suiters.

SOUTH	WEST	NORTH	EAST
1 N T	Pass	2 ♠	Pass
2 N T	Pass	3 (Sign-off)	

South should pass. If South had raised, North could pass.

SOUTH	WEST	NORTH	EAST
1 N T	Pass	2 ♡	Pass
2 N T	Pass	3 ♢ (Weak)	

South should usually pass or show preference.

RESPONSES TO ONE NOTRUMP

Situation: Partner opened one notrump.

In the chart below it is assumed that the Stayman convention (page 36) is being used. Any suit take-out of two, except two clubs, is nonforcing and weak, inviting a pass. Among players who do not use Stayman, any nonjump suit takeout is forcing for one round, as it would be over a suit-bid.

With a 6-card minor headed by A-Q or A-K (such as ◇ A-K-7-5-4-2) or with a solid 5-card minor (◇ A-K-Q-6-3), RAISE THE NOTRUMP—even if an opponent has overcalled and you have no stopper in his suit.

With 4-3-3-3 distribution, and with a 4-4-3-2 or 5-3-3-2 hand lacking a 4-card or longer major, it is best to raise the notrump bid if able. *Count high-card points only.*

POINTS	RESPONSE
0 to 3	Usually, PASS. But bid TWO in a 6-card suit; bid FOUR in an 8-card major.
4 to 7	Usually, PASS. But bid a 5-card suit (except clubs) with unbalanced distribution; bid FOUR in a major with a 6-card or longer suit and 6 winners or more in the hand.
8 or 9	RAISE to 2 N T STAYMAN response (2 ♣) if able BID FOUR in a major, as above
10 to 14	RAISE to 3 N T STAYMAN response (2♣) if able JUMP TO THREE in a long suit (forcing to game)
15 or 16	RAISE to 4 N T—or make a Stayman response or jump takeout
17 or 18	RAISE to 5 N T—or make a Stayman response or jump takeout
19 or 20	RAISE to 6 N T—or make a Stayman response or jump takeout
21	RAISE to 7 N T

POINT-COUNT VALUATION

BIDDABLE SUITS

OPENING ONE-BIDS

CHOICE OF SUITS

FORCING BIDS

RESPONSES TO SUIT-BIDS

OPENER'S REBIDS

RESPONDER'S REBIDS

NOTRUMP BIDDING

OPENING 3, 4, 5 BIDS

FORCING TWO-BIDS

OVERCALLS

TAKEOUT DOUBLE

PENALTY DOUBLES

PART-SCORE

DUPLICATE

SLAM BIDS

4-5 NOTRUMP SLAM BIDS

BIDDING CONVENTIONS

PERCENTAGE TABLES

BIDDING SYSTEMS

OPENING LEADS

SIGNALS IN PLAY

COVERING HONORS

FINESSES

SAFETY PLAYS

END-PLAYS SQUEEZE

BRIDGE LAWS

GLOSSARY

NOTRUMP BIDDING
The Stayman Convention

The Stayman Convention is a method of responding to partner's opening notrump bid so as to find a possible 4-4 (or better) major suit. Nearly all advanced and expert players use Stayman.

There are "forcing Stayman" and "nonforcing Stayman," the latter being more popular. In forcing Stayman a contract of two notrump, or higher, must be reached. In nonforcing Stayman the bidding may end at two of a major, if the opening bid was one notrump. If the opening bid was two notrump, the Stayman response is forcing to game.

"Modified" or "extended" Stayman, employing two-diamond responses for special purposes, are used by some tournament players. They are covered on page 38.

Over Partner's One Notrump

1. A response of two clubs is forcing. It does not promise a club suit.
2. Opener must rebid two (never more) in a 4-card major suit if he has one. (Some players require that the suit be at least Q-x-x-x or J-10-x-x.) With 4-card suits in both majors, opener rebids two spades.
3. Opener's rebid must be two diamonds if he cannot show a 4-card major suit. (This rebid does not promise diamond strength.)
4. Responder may pass any rebid by opener, including two diamonds.
5. If responder rebids two spades or two hearts he shows a 5-card or longer suit. Opener may raise with 3-card support, show a second 4-card major, or bid two notrump. (In forcing Stayman he may not pass.)
6. If responder rebids three clubs he shows a 6-card club suit and a weak hand. Opener must pass.
7. If responder rebids three diamonds, hearts, or spades, it is forcing to game. (He may bid three diamonds without a diamond suit.)
8. If responder's first response is two spades, hearts, or diamonds, he shows a weak hand with a 5-card or longer suit. *Opener should usually pass* but may raise responder's suit to three with A-K-x, A-Q-x or K-Q-x in responder's suit and at least 17 points.

NOTRUMP BIDDING
The Stayman Convention (Continued)

9. After opener's rebid, responder may raise a major to three or four, bid two notrump (8 or 9 points), or bid three notrump or more (10 or more points).
10. A jump to four clubs is Gerber (page 66).

Requirements for the two-club response. The responder may bid two clubs on a weak hand (3 to 7 points), intending to pass or sign off at his next turn, if he thinks a major-suit contract will be safer than a notrump contract. There is no top limit to the strength shown by the two-club response, since it is forcing.

South	West	North	East
1 N T	Pass	2 ♣	Pass
2 ◇	Pass		

North's rebid will be, holding:

♠ 10-8-6-4	♡ 9-3	◇ K-10-7-5-3	♣ 6-5	Pass
♠ Q-7-5-3	♡ 6	◇ 6-2	♣ Q-10-9-7-6-3	Three clubs
♠ Q-J-8-5-4	♡ 7-5-3-2	◇ J-3	♣ 7-2	Two spades
♠ J-10-6-3	♡ K-9-7-2	◇ A-6-3	♣ 5-4	Two notrump
♠ Q-7	♡ K-Q-10-6	◇ A-5-4	♣ 7-6-5-3	Three notrump
♠ Q-6-5-3	♡ A-Q-8-7-4	◇ 8-4-3	♣ 6	Three hearts
♠ 2	♡ Q-J-6-3	◇ A-K-10-7	♣ Q-7-6-2	Three diamonds

South	West	North	East
1 N T	Pass	2 ♣	Pass
2 ♠	Pass		

North's rebid will be, holding:

♠ 10-8-6-4	♡ 9-3	◇ K-10-7-5-3	♣ 6-5	Pass
♠ Q-7-5-3	♡ 6	◇ 6-2	♣ Q-10-9-7-6-3	Four spades
♠ J-10-6-3	♡ K-9-7-2	◇ A-6-3	♣ 5-4	Four spades
♠ 6	♡ Q-J-6-3	◇ A-K-10-7	♣ Q-7-6-2	Three diamonds

Over Partner's Two-Notrump Opening

1. A response of three clubs is forcing to game. It does not promise a club suit.
2. Opener must rebid three (never more) in a 4-card major suit, preferring spades. Lacking a 4-card major, he bids three diamonds.
3. Responder's rebid of four in a major or three notrump must be passed. Responder's rebid of three in a major must be raised with 3-card support. Responder's rebid of four clubs (not Gerber) or four diamonds shows a genuine suit.
4. An original jump response of four clubs is Gerber; in any other suit it is a slam try showing a long suit and strong hand (about 10 pts.).

South	West	North	East
2 N T	Pass	3 ♣	

North may hold:

1. ♠ Q-10-8-4   ♡ K-9-5-2   ◇ 8-4-3   ♣ 9-5
North will raise 3 ♡ or 3 ♠ to four and will bid 3 N T over 3 ◇.

2. ♠ K-7-5-4-3   ♡ 9-5   ◇ A-10-8-6-5   ♣ 4
North will bid 4 ◇ over 3 ♠; 3 N T over 3 ◇; 3 ♠ over 3 ♡ (and pass a 3 N T rebid).

POINT-COUNT VALUATION
BIDDABLE SUITS
OPENING ONE-BIDS
CHOICE OF SUITS
FORCING BIDS
RESPONSES TO SUIT-BIDS
OPENER'S REBIDS
RESPONDER'S REBIDS
NOTRUMP BIDDING
OPENING 3, 4, 5 BIDS
FORCING TWO-BIDS
OVERCALLS
TAKEOUT DOUBLE
PENALTY DOUBLES
PART-SCORE
DUPLICATE
SLAM BIDS
4-5 NOTRUMP SLAM BIDS
BIDDING CONVENTIONS
PERCENTAGE TABLES
BIDDING SYSTEMS
OPENING LEADS
SIGNALS IN PLAY
COVERING HONORS
FINESSES
SAFETY PLAYS
END-PLAYS SQUEEZE
BRIDGE LAWS
GLOSSARY

OPTIONAL RESPONSES TO 1 N T
Modified or Extended Stayman

The many variations of the Stayman Convention (page 36) have two main branches: (1) use of 2 ◇, as well as 2 ♣, as a forcing response to 1 N T; (2) special meanings given to certain rebids. Some of the principal variations are:

WEAK AND STRONG RESPONSES. Either 2 ♣ or 2 ◇ asks for a major-suit response, but 2 ♣ shows 9 pts. or less and is not forcing; 2 ◇ shows 10 pts. or more and is forcing to game.

ASKING FOR BETTER MAJOR. A 2 ♣ response requires opener to rebid in a 4-card major; a 2 ◇ response shows at least one 5-card major in the responding hand, probably two 5-card majors, and requires opener to bid his longer or better major, even if it is only a 3-card holding.

MURRAY CONVENTION. (Eric Murray of Toronto.) A 2 ◇ response requires opener to show his best major, as in the preceding paragraph. Responder's rebid at the three-level is invitational but not forcing. If responder's rebid is 2 N T, opener must show his 4-card suit(s), beginning with the lowest.

REBID TO SHOW BOTH MAJORS. *By Opener:* Over the Stayman response, a rebid of 3 ♣ by opener shows that he has two 4-card majors. *By Responder:* After the Stayman response and opener's 2 ◇ rebid, a certain rebid by responder (3 ♣, 3 ◇, or 2 N T, depending on the system being used) requires opener to show now his longer or better major.

OPENER'S REBID TO DEFINE HIS HAND. Over the 2 ♣ response, opener (lacking a 4-card major) rebids 2 ◇ with a minimum notrump and 2 N T with a maximum. This was part of the original Stayman Convention. It has been abandoned by most experts but still is widely used.

PREEMPTIVE RESPONSES. Any jump to three of a suit over partner's opening 1 N T bid is weak and demands that opener pass.

FLINT CONVENTION. (Jeremy Flint of England.) Over an opening 2 N T, a 3 ◇ response requires opener to bid 3 ♡. The 3 ◇ response is designed for weak hands, such as

♠ 8-7   ♡ 10-8-5-4-3-2   ◇ J-7-3   ♣ 10-2

Responder will pass 3 ♡. If his suit were spades, he will bid 3 ♠ and opener must pass. If he has a strong hand, or a diamond suit, he can continue bidding to game or beyond.

OPTIONAL N T BIDDING (Cont'd)
Transfer Bids ("Texas")

Transfer bids are based on the fact that there usually is an advantage if the stronger of the partnership hands is declarer. Europeans call transfer bids "Texas" (the Texas convention) because the convention originated in the U. S. Southwest. It is credited to David Carter.

When the bidding is opened with one notrump and the responder has a hand justifying a jump to four of a major (page 35), the responder bids

4 ◊ if his suit is hearts

4 ♡ if his suit is spades

The opener *must* then bid four in the suit next-higher than the response, and the responder must then pass.

SOUTH	WEST	NORTH	EAST	*North has:*	
1 N T	Pass	4 ◊	Pass	♠	7-6
4 ♡				♡	K-10-8-7-6-2
				◊	8-4-3
				♣	K-8

SOUTH	WEST	NORTH	EAST	*North has:*	
1 N T	Pass	4 ♡	Pass	♠	K-J-8-7-5-4-2
4 ♠				♡	6
				◊	Q-5-3
				♣	8-4

A four-club response is the Gerber Convention (page 66). A four-spade response (seldom used) requires a five-club bid.

See also Jacoby Transfer Bids, page 77

The Weak Notrump

An opening one-notrump bid is called "weak" when it contains fewer than 15 pts. In the Kaplan-Sheinwold System (page 90) a weak notrump of 11 to 14 pts. is used. Some systems use a 12- to 14-pt. or 12- to 15-pt. range if the 15-point hand does not have "body"—several tens or nines not included in the point-count.

Examples of the weak notrump;

1.	♠ K-7-3	♡ Q-10-7-5	◊ A-8-2	♣ K-J-7	13 pts.
2.	♠ K-Q-6-3	♡ K-8-7-5	◊ J-6-4	♣ A-J	14 pts.
3.	♠ 8-2	♡ A-Q-6	◊ K-9-4-3	♣ Q-J-8-3	12 pts.

Many players use the weak notrump only when not vulnerable. When vulnerable they require 16 or more points.

Responses to the weak notrump are based on the Table of Expectancies on page 3. The responder raises to 2 N T if the combined hands *may* have 26 pts. and to 3 N T if they surely have 26 pts., or makes a forcing response. The Stayman Convention is used.

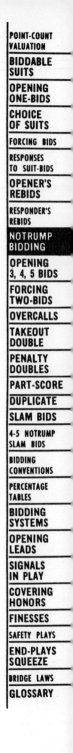

REBIDS BY NOTRUMP BIDDER

Situation: You opened the bidding with one notrump (16 to 18 points). Your partner responded. You should rebid (or pass) as follows.

REBIDS BY ONE-NOTRUMP BIDDER

RESPONSE	THE OPENER SHOULD NOW
A RAISE TO TWO NOTRUMP	Pass only with 16 points or less and one suit unstopped BID a biddable 4-card major (if not using Stayman) BID three notrump
THREE NOTRUMP OR FOUR IN A MAJOR	PASS—the responder has decided no slam is possible
TWO IN A SUIT	PASS if using Stayman; if not: RAISE a major with 4 trumps BID a 4-card biddable major RAISE partner's suit with K-Q-x, A-Q-x or A-K-x BID two notrump
THREE IN A SUIT	*Do not pass short of game* RAISE a major with 4 trumps BID *three* in a biddable suit BID three notrump

REBIDS BY TWO-NOTRUMP BIDDER

Any response is forcing to game—DO NOT PASS.

BID A 4-CARD MAJOR over a Stayman response; bid three diamonds lacking a 4-card major.

With 24 points, bid 6 N T over a raise to 4 N T (NOT Blackwood); with 23 points, bid 6 N T over a raise to 5 N T; with less, PASS. *Do not bid 7 N T.*

RAISE partner's major-suit takeout to four with four trumps or at least K-x-x in partner's suit.

BID THREE NOTRUMP with any other hand.

REBIDS BY THREE-NOTRUMP BIDDER

Any response to an opening three-notrump bid is a slam try. A response is *not forcing* (except 4 ♣ or 4 ♦, when not enough for game) and the opener should pass unless he has 27 points, or 26 points including three Aces, or 25 points including strong support for partner's suit and at least two Aces. A 4 N T bid by the responder or a 4 N T rebid by the opener is NOT Blackwood (see page 63).

SACRIFICE BIDDING

Making game (including the trick-score) is worth about 500 points. Therefore it is always profitable to overbid and go down 300 points or less *when you are sure the opponents can make a game*. But never go down more than 500 points to prevent an opposing game.

Opening preëmptive or shut-out bids and defenders' overcalls are based on the Rule of 2 and 3.

Vulnerability conditions can influence sacrifice bidding. When vulnerable against nonvulnerable opponents, you need one winner more; when you are not vulnerable against vulnerable opponents, you need one winner less. The following table assumes equal vulnerability.

THE RULE OF TWO AND THREE

When the opponents are bidding, and partner has passed or has made no bid, do not bid unless you can win, in your own hand,

Within **2** tricks of your contract if VULNERABLE

Within **3** tricks of your contract if NOT VULNERABLE

Then you cannot be set more than 500 points

How to Count Winners

To know whether a bid will be safe, under the Rule of 2 and 3, at your own suit-bid, estimate winners as follows (keeping in mind the importance of a good trump suit):

1. Count your honor-tricks (page 4) except that a third honor in any suit is given its full playing value. For instance, A-K-Q is counted as three and K-Q-J as two winners (or tricks).

2. Count your long-suit winners, according to the following formula: 1 winner for every card over *four* in the trump suit; and 1 winner for every card over *three* in each side suit.

With a solid or nearly solid suit, simply count each missing higher honor (A, K or Q) as a sure or probable loser.

Add honor and length winners for the total trick-winning value of the trump suit and the opening hand.

OPENING 3-, 4-, AND 5-BIDS

An opening bid of three or four in a suit (and an opening bid of five in a minor) shows a long, powerful trump suit but is *weaker than a one-bid* in high cards. These are preëmptive bids. Their purpose is to shut the opponents out of the bidding.

A preëmptive bid should not usually include more than 10 high-card points. However, an odd jack or queen in J-x-x or Q-x is not counted.

Every preëmptive bid is based on the Rule of 2 and 3 (page 41) and is an intentional overbid. A preëmptive bid should not be made fourth hand without fair expectancy of making the contract.

AN OPENING THREE-BID REQUIRES

A strong 6-card or 7-card suit, in a hand with 7 winners if vulnerable,

6 to 7 not vulnerable

A minor-suit three-bid should usually be made on a suit headed by K-Q, A-Q or better, so that partner with a good hand and the missing top card may bid three notrump.

Examples of opening three-bids, vulnerable:
1. ♠ 8   ♡ Q-J-8-7-6-5-3   ◇ K-Q-10-9   ♣ 5 Three hearts
2. ♠ 6-3   ♡ 5   ◇ Q-J-10   ♣ K-Q-J-8-6-5-3 Three clubs

Not vulnerable:
3. ♠ K-J-10-9-6-4-2   ♡ 3   ◇ J-10-9-6   ♣ 8 Three spades

AN OPENING FOUR-BID REQUIRES

A strong 7-card, or any 8-card suit, in a hand with 8 winners if vulnerable,

7 to 8 not vulnerable

An opening four-bid seldom has as many as 2½ honor-tricks (with which a one-bid would be preferred).

Examples of opening four-bids:
1. ♠ 6   ♡ A-K-Q-J-9-7-6-3   ◇ 6-5-3   ♣ 7   Four hearts
2. ♠ 8-5   ♡ —   ◇ K-Q-J-2   ♣ Q-J-10-9-7-6-4 Four clubs

A PREËMPTIVE BID OF 5 ◇ OR 5 ♣ is almost always doubled if the opponents have superior cards. It requires 9 winners whether or not vulnerable, nearly always an 8-card or longer suit, and a freakish hand, for example:

♠ 6   ♡ —   ◇ A-Q-J-9-7-6-5-4   ♣ Q-J-10-8   Bid 5 ◇
♣ —   ♡ 6-5-2   ◇ 8   ♣ A-K-9-8-7-6-5-3-2   Bid 5 ♣

See also the weak two-bid, page 46.

RESPONSES TO 3-, 4-, 5-BIDS

Only aces, kings, ruffing tricks and trump length may be counted as tricks in support of partner's preëmptive bid.

In general, you may raise a preëmptive bid once for every supporting winner over 2, if vulnerable, and over 3, if not vulnerable.

Before raising, consider a penalty double (page 56).

How to Respond

DO NOT RAISE a major-suit four-bid except as a sacrifice bid (if the opponents overcall) or as a slam try (if you have 18 pts. or more, including three aces, or two aces and a king, with some support for partner's suit).

A 3-, 4- or 5-bid shows a trump suit strong enough to play without support. You may raise with a singleton in partner's suit, if necessary.

IN DOUBLING, do not depend on partner for any defensive tricks.

BID THREE NOTRUMP over a minor-suit three-bid with stoppers in the other three suits plus at least A-x, K-x or Q-x in partner's suit (or one of these combinations with 9 points outside). Bid three in a very strong rebiddable major suit with 12 points.

Partner opens with three clubs.
1. ♠ J-8-7-3   ♡ Q-J-7   ◇ A-7-6-3   ♣ A-6   Three notrump
2. ♠ K-Q-10-9-7-6   ♡ 7-2   ◇ A-Q-10   ♣ 6-3   Three spades

Count of Supporting Winners

In support of partner's preëmptive bid, count:

1. Honor-tricks at their defensive value only, except count 1 winner for king or queen of partner's suit.

2. Long cards in *partner's trump suit only*: ½ trick for a 4-card length, 1 trick for a 5-card length.

3. Ruffing tricks, as follows:

RUFFING WINNERS		
With two short suits, count only one —the shorter	*With 3 trumps*	*With 4 or more trumps*
Doubleton	½ trick	1 trick
Singleton	1 trick	2 tricks
Void	2 tricks	3 tricks

Defense against opponents' preëmptive bids: See page 74.

POINT-COUNT VALUATION
BIDDABLE SUITS
OPENING ONE-BIDS
CHOICE OF SUITS
FORCING BIDS
RESPONSES TO SUIT-BIDS
OPENER'S REBIDS
RESPONDER'S REBIDS
NOTRUMP BIDDING
OPENING 3, 4, 5 BIDS
FORCING TWO-BIDS
OVERCALLS
TAKEOUT DOUBLE
PENALTY DOUBLES
PART-SCORE
DUPLICATE
SLAM BIDS
4-5 NOTRUMP SLAM BIDS
BIDDING CONVENTIONS
PERCENTAGE TABLES
BIDDING SYSTEMS
OPENING LEADS
SIGNALS IN PLAY
COVERING HONORS
FINESSES
SAFETY PLAYS
END-PLAYS SQUEEZE
BRIDGE LAWS
GLOSSARY

THE FORCING TWO-BID

The opening bid of two in a suit is the strongest bid in bridge. After a forcing two-bid, neither partner may let the bidding die short of game (except to make or pass a penalty double).

The two-bid is based chiefly on honor- or quick tricks, plus at least one strong suit (in top cards), plus controls (page 60). Usually a two-bid should show at least second-round control (king or singleton) in *every* suit.

Requirements

5½ to 6 honor-tricks—usually **25 points** or more—with a strong 4- or 5-card biddable suit (headed by A-K, K-Q-J or better).

♠ A-K-6   ♡ A-Q-J-6   ◇ A-K-Q-8-3   ♣ 3   Two diamonds

5 honor-tricks—usually **23 points** or more—with two strong 5-card or longer suits or a solid 6-card suit.

♠ K-Q-J-8-3   ♡ A-K-Q-10-5   ◇ A-Q   ♣ 6   Two spades
♠ A-K   ♡ K-Q-J-10-6-3   ◇ A-Q-J   ♣ 4-2   Two hearts

4½ honor-tricks—usually **21 points** or more—with a solid 7-card suit. (With an 8-card suit 4 to 4+ honor-tricks are enough.)

♠ A-J-3   ♡ A-5   ◇ A-K-Q-8-6-5-3   ♣ 6   Two diamonds
♠ A-K-10-9-7-6-3-2   ♡ A-5   ◇ A-4   ♣ 6   Two spades

The Two-Club Bid

In several systems and among many players the only opening forcing bid is *two clubs,* as follows:

1. An opening two-club bid is artificial, not necessarily showing club strength, and is forcing.
2. Partner must respond two diamonds if he has less than an ace and a king, or less than 7 points in high cards. With this much strength or more, partner responds with a raise or suit or notrump takeout, as he would to a one-bid.
3. If opener's rebid is *two notrump,* it shows a regular two-notrump hand and responder passes or responds as he would if the opening bid had been two notrump (page 28).
4. If opener's rebid is anything but two notrump, a game-forcing situation exists.
5. Opening two-bids in spades, hearts, or diamonds may be strong (page 47) or weak (page 46).

Typical artificial, forcing two-club bids:

♠ A-K-6   ♡ A-Q-J-6   ◇ A-10-7   ♣ K-J-7   Two clubs
♣ A-K-10-8-6-3   ♡ 6   ◇ A-K-Q-8   ♣ A-5   Two clubs

RESPONSES TO TWO-BIDS

When your partner opens with a forcing two-bid and the intervening opponent passes, *do not pass.* Generally speaking, you respond as you would to a one-bid, but at a level one trick higher: If you would raise a one-bid, raise a two-bid; bid a suit, if you would bid it over a one-bid.

To an artificial forcing two-club bid, unless the response must be two diamonds (page 44), the positive responses are the same.

YOU HOLD	RESPONSE TO A TWO-BID
0 to **5** pts.	BID TWO NOTRUMP, or two diamonds over two clubs
6 points	RAISE once with 3 trumps and a singleton, or 4 trumps and a doubleton BID TWO in a higher-ranking suit With less, bid TWO NO-TRUMP (two diamonds over two clubs)
7 points	BID a biddable suit RAISE with adequate support BID THREE NOTRUMP (two notrump over two clubs)
8 points or more	BID a biddable suit, or RAISE with adequate support but TRY FOR A SLAM later

The Warning Double Raise

If you are *sure* your partner understands its meaning, give partner an immediate double raise (to four) holding five trumps (or Q-x-x-x in trumps) with *no ace, king, singleton or void* in your hand.

If An Opponent Overcalls

Pass if your response would have been two notrump; otherwise respond as you would have, or double for penalties. A free notrump response requires a stopper in the opponent's suit.

Ace-Showing Responses

These are played by some experts. There are various methods, described on page 47.

TWO-BID CONVENTIONS

Two-club and Two-diamond Convention

In several variations of the two-club forcing bid (page 44), two diamonds also is a forcing bid.

TWO CLUBS—forcing for one round. Negative response is two diamonds. (Any positive response is forcing to game.) If over two diamonds opener's rebid is two notrump, he shows a 22-to-24 pt. notrump hand; if his rebid is a suit he shows a strong suit or two-suiter. Neither bid is forcing.

Examples:

♠ A-Q-6	♡ K-10-4	◇ A-K-Q-7	♣ K-J-3	Two clubs
♠ K-Q-J-10-8-4	♡ 6-3	◇ A-K-5	♣ A-3	Two clubs
♠ —	♡ K-Q-J-10-6-3	◇ A-K-Q-10-5	♣ 4-3	Two clubs

TWO DIAMONDS—forcing to game. Negative response is two hearts but ace-showing responses (page 47) are used by most players. Usually at least 23 pts. in high cards and no less than second-round control in any suit.

Examples:

| ♠ A-K-Q-3 | ♡ K-Q-10-9 | ◇ A-K-5-4 | ♣ A | Two diamonds |
| ♠ A-K-J-5 | ♡ A | ◇ 6 | ♣ A-K-Q-8-7-5-3 | Two diamonds |

Two-club and two-diamond conventions are used with either the weak or the intermediate two-bid.

Weak Two-bids

The weak two-bid is a preëmptive bid, with rigid requirements in high cards.*

An opening bid of two in spades, hearts, or diamonds (unless a two-diamond bid is used as forcing) shows:

> **A fairly strong 6-card suit**
> **About 8 pts., 1½ quick tricks**
> **(less than enough for a one-bid)**
> **½ to 1 quick trick outside the trump suit**

Examples:

♠ K-J-9-6-5-3	♡ 6-2	◇ A-9-5	♣ 8-3	Two spades
♠ 6	♡ Q-10-9-8-3-2	◇ 7-5	♣ A-Q-6-2	Two hearts
♠ 5-4	♡ K-8	◇ A-J-10-7-5-4	♣ 6-5-3	Two diamonds

RESPONSES. A weak two-bid may be passed; partner should seldom try for game without 16 pts. or more. *Any raise is preëmptive,* showing trump support but defensive weakness. With most players, *two notrump is the ONLY forcing response,* but some treat any suit takeout as forcing.

REBIDS. A rebid in the same suit by the opener shows a minimum. A rebid in a new suit shows that the hand is relatively good (for a weak two-bid) and locates the hand's outside strength.

---

*In American tournaments, 6 to 12 high-card points.

TWO-BID CONVENTIONS (Cont'd)
Intermediate Two-bids

In some systems in which the artificial forcing two-bid is used (including the Acol System—page 86), an opening bid of two spades, hearts or diamonds shows a strong but not game-forcing hand. It is used on two types of hand:

(a) Playing strength that warrants game, but not enough in high cards for a two-club bid.

♠ 6	♡ K-Q-J-8-7-3	◇ A-K-Q-6-5	♣ 4	Two hearts
♣ A	♡ 6-3	◇ A-K-Q-9-7-6-5-2	♣ Q-3	Two diamonds

(b) Enough in high cards for a two-club bid, but too little in playing strength to force to game.

♠ A-Q-7-6-3	♡ A-K-5-4-2	◇ A-Q	♣ 6	Two spades
♣ A-K-6-2	♡ 6	◇ A-K-5-4	♣ A-K-6-3	Two diamonds

RESPONSES. Responder may pass a hopeless hand. A response of two notrump shows a weak hand but gives the opener a chance to bid a second suit, which responder may be able to raise but may pass. *Any other response is forcing to game.*

Partner opens two hearts (intermediate two-bid).

♠ K-6-3-2	♡ 7-4	◇ 8-6-2	♣ 8-7-6-3	Pass
♣ 10-7-5-3	♡ 8	◇ K-8-5-2	♣ Q-7-6-3	Two notrump
♣ 8-5-4	♡ J-7-6	◇ A-8-7-5-3	♣ 8-7	Three hearts
♣ K-Q-10-8-6-4	♡ 6-3	◇ 7-5	♣ K-7-6	Two spades

Ace-Showing Responses to Two-bids

Ace-showing responses may be used over either forcing two-bids or the two-club bid and are an integral part of some systems (see CAB, page 87). There are many variations. The following are among the most popular.

OVER A FORCING TWO-BID. With one ace, bid the suit of the ace; with the ace *or* king of partner's suit, raise to three. With two aces, jump to 4 N T. Lacking any ace, respond 2 N T, *EXCEPT:* Jump to 3 N T with two kings or with 7 or more points including a K-Q; jump one trick in a strong suit such as K-Q-J-x-x-x and an aceless hand.

OVER THE ARTIFICIAL TWO-CLUB BID. With the ♠ A, bid 2 ♠; ♡ A, 2 ♡; ◇ A, 3 ◇; ♣ A, 3 ♣. Bid 3 N T with any two aces; 2 N T with no ace but two kings. On any other hand respond 2 ◇.

KING-SHOWING. This is an extension of ace-showing, not so often played. *The responder's second response, if in a new suit, shows the king of the suit in which he responds.*

Example:

	SOUTH	WEST	NORTH	EAST
	2 ♡	Pass	2 ♠ *or* 2 N T	Pass
	3 ♡	Pass	4 ◇ *(showing ◇ K)*	
			but 4 ♡ *(heart raise)*	

POINT-COUNT VALUATION

BIDDABLE SUITS

OPENING ONE-BIDS

CHOICE OF SUITS

FORCING BIDS

RESPONSES TO SUIT-BIDS

OPENER'S REBIDS

RESPONDER'S REBIDS

NOTRUMP BIDDING

OPENING 3, 4, 5 BIDS

FORCING TWO-BIDS

OVERCALLS

TAKEOUT DOUBLE

PENALTY DOUBLES

PART-SCORE

DUPLICATE

SLAM BIDS

4-5 NOTRUMP SLAM BIDS

BIDDING CONVENTIONS

PERCENTAGE TABLES

BIDDING SYSTEMS

OPENING LEADS

SIGNALS IN PLAY

COVERING HONORS

FINESSES

SAFETY PLAYS

END-PLAYS SQUEEZE

BRIDGE LAWS

GLOSSARY

BIDS BY THE DEFENDERS

During the auction, the defenders are the two members of the side that did not open the bidding.

A defender has several incentives to enter the auction: To outbid the opponents and make a part-score or game; to find a good sacrifice contract; or to guide partner to the best opening lead. But a defender should not bid unless he is safe under the Rule of 2 and 3 (page 41). A defender should not bid a doubtful hand if his suit is weak in high cards and he does not wish to have his partner lead it.

The following table lists standard defenders' bids, detailed requirements for which are listed on the following pages. In addition there are several popular conventional overcalls described on pages 70 through 75.

HOLDING	YOU SHOULD
9 points or less	*Usually,* PASS; but BID ONE in a long suit, if able (page 49), or PREEMPTIVE JUMP OVERCALL (page 50)
10 to **14** points	OVERCALL if able (page 49) TAKEOUT DOUBLE (rarely) PREEMPTIVE JUMP OVERCALL
15 to **18** points	TAKEOUT DOUBLE (page 41) JUMP OVERCALL (page 51) ONE NOTRUMP with a sure stopper in opponents' suit(s)
19 points or more	*Usually,* TAKEOUT DOUBLE OVERCALL IN OPPONENT'S SUIT, or NOTRUMP OVERCALL (forcing)

DEFENDERS' OVERCALLS

Before overcalling, count your winners and make sure you are safe under the Rule of 2 and 3 (page 34). It is not enough to have the equivalent of an opening bid. The suit must be strong, especially at the level of two or higher.

The following chart lists non-jump overcalls. A jump overcall may be strong (page 51) or preëmptive (page 42).

OVER-CALL	REQUIRES
ONE IN A SUIT	5 winners vulnerable, 4 not vulnerable *Usually,* 7 pts. with a 5-card suit 10 pts. with a 4-card suit
TWO IN A SUIT	6 winners vulnerable, 5 not vulnerable *Usually,* 7 pts. with a 6-card suit 10 points with a strong 5-card suit Do not bid a 4-card suit
THREE IN A SUIT	7 winners vulnerable, 6 nonvulnerable 9 to 15 pts. with a 6-card or longer suit
ONE NO-TRUMP (or more)	About 16 to 18 pts. (about the same as an opening notrump bid) but including a stopper in the opponent's suit. A jump overcall of two notrump is the unusual notrump (page 56). A non-jump overcall of two or three notrump is based on the tricks the bidder expects to win.

Prefer a takeout double when strong enough.

Responses to Overcalls

It is not desirable to keep the bidding open on a weak hand.

RAISE once for each supporting winner over 2 if vulnerable, or 3, if not vulnerable, including at least 1½ honor-tricks and adequate trump support.

BID NOTRUMP with about 10 pts. including a double stopper in the opponents' suit.

BID A SUIT if your own hand is strong enough for an overcall.

JUMP ONE TRICK in a new suit (*forcing for one round*) with 11 to 15 pts., including a strong suit of your own or support for partner's suit.

DEFENDERS' OVERCALLS (Cont'd)

Preëmptive Overcalls

A *double-jump overcall* (as three spades over opponent's one heart, or four clubs over opponent's one heart) is a preëmptive bid subject to the rules given for opening preëmptive bids (page 42).

A *single-jump overcall* (as two spades over opponent's one heart, or three clubs over opponent's one heart) is used by some players as preëmptive (page 42) and by others as a strength-showing bid (page 51).

Opponent opened one heart.
Examples of preëmptive jump overcalls:

♠ K-J-10-8-7-6-3	♡ 7	◊ 8	♣ Q-10-8-6	Three spades
♠ 7-6	♡ 5-2	◊ 8	♣ A-K-Q-10-8-7-6-3	Four clubs

Reopening the Bidding

When the opponents stop short of game, and a pass by the last player would leave them to play at a part-score, a bid or double by that player may be made on less strength than is required in other circumstances.

SOUTH	WEST	NORTH	EAST
1 ♡	Pass	Pass	

SOUTH	WEST	NORTH	EAST
1 ◊	Pass	1 ♡	Pass
1 N T	Pass	2 ♡	Pass
Pass			

East's bid, holding:

♠ Q-8-7-5-3	♠ Q-8-7-5
♡ J-7-6	♡ J-7
◊ A-8	◊ A-10-8-2
♣ K-5-4	♣ K-J-3
One spade	Double

West's bid, holding:

♠ Q-8-7-5-3	♠ J-9-6-5
♡ 10-5	♡ 7-2
◊ K-7	◊ K-7
♣ A-Q-6-2	♣ A-K-8-5-4
Two spades	Double

A jump overcall is used to show an opening bid or better, including a strong suit, in the first situation.

♠ K-Q-10-7-3   ♡ A-7   ◊ 6-2   ♣ A-9-6-3   Two spades

The act of reopening the bidding against an opposing part-score bid is called *balancing* and is based on the assumption that partner has some high-card strength. From the total of 40 points in the pack (page 3) deduct the probable 20 to 22 points that the opponents usually hold when they stop at a part-score of one or two, then deduct the points you hold, and partner must have the remainder. This principle, though essential to good bidding, is dangerous if applied too optimistically.

The Trap Pass

With length and strength in the opponent's suit, it is better to pass on the first round than to overcall.

South opens one heart. West holds:

♠ K-Q-10-3   ♡ A-J-8-6-3   ◊ K-6   ♣ 8-2   Pass

STRENGTH-SHOWING OVERCALLS
The Jump Overcall (not forcing)

As used by most players, a single jump overcall (one trick more than necessary, as two spades over opponent's one diamond, or three diamonds over opponent's one heart) *shows a strong hand but is not forcing*. Requirements are:

14 to 16 points (3 to 3½ **quick tricks**) in high cards, and
Two strong 5-card or longer suits; or
One strong major suit or solid minor suit of at least six cards.

An opponent opens with one diamond. Proper overcall:
1. ♠ A-K-10-5-4 ♡ A-Q-J-7-5 ◇ 6 ♣ 3-2 Two spades
2. ♠ K-Q-J-8-7-5-3 ♡ A-6 ◇ A-5-3 ♣ 4 Two spades

An opponent opens with one spade. Proper overcall:
3. ♠ 6 ♡ A-K-10-9-8-7-5 ◇ A-J-10 ♣ K-9 Three hearts
4. ♠ 6 ♡ A-3 ◇ A-K-Q-10-7-4-3 ♣ 8-6-2 Three diamonds

The jump overcall invites a weak response:
RAISE a jump overcall with about 1 honor-trick or more and x-x-x or better in trumps;
BID NOTRUMP with 8 high-card points or more including a sure stopper in the opponents' suit.
TAKE OUT in a rebiddable *major* suit or in any strong rebiddable suit with 1½ or more quick tricks.
PASS with less.

The Immediate Overcall (forcing)

When an opponent opens the bidding and your hand would—or almost would—justify an opening (game-forcing) two-bid, you show your strength by overcalling at your first opportunity in the opponent's suit. This overcall usually shows first-round control (ace or void) and at least second-round control (singleton or king) in the opponent's suit; with two or three smaller cards in the opponent's suit a takeout double is preferred.

Over an opponent's opening one-club bid:
1. ♠ K-Q-10-6 ♡ A-K-Q-5-4 ◇ K-J-10-6 ♣ — Two clubs
2. ♠ A-K-Q-10-5-4-2 ♡ A-Q-J ◇ K-Q ♣ 3 Two clubs

This overcall is forcing for one round but may be dropped short of game.

When the opponent's bid is a preëmptive four-bid, such a hand is shown by bidding FOUR NOTRUMP (not an ace-showing slam try); when the opponents' bid is a preëmptive five-bid, the proper overcall is FIVE NOTRUMP. These are forcing bids.

All these bids are gigantic takeout doubles. Partner responds by showing his best suit

See also the unusual notrump, page 70.

POINT-COUNT VALUATION

BIDDABLE SUITS

OPENING ONE-BIDS

CHOICE OF SUITS

FORCING BIDS

RESPONSES TO SUIT-BIDS

OPENER'S REBIDS

RESPONDER'S REBIDS

NOTRUMP BIDDING

OPENING 3, 4, 5 BIDS

FORCING TWO-BIDS

OVERCALLS

TAKEOUT DOUBLE

PENALTY DOUBLES

PART-SCORE

DUPLICATE

SLAM BIDS

4-5 NOTRUMP SLAM BIDS

BIDDING CONVENTIONS

PERCENTAGE TABLES

BIDDING SYSTEMS

OPENING LEADS

SIGNALS IN PLAY

COVERING HONORS

FINESSES

SAFETY PLAYS

END-PLAYS SQUEEZE

BRIDGE LAWS

GLOSSARY

THE TAKEOUT DOUBLE

A takeout double is a convention that asks partner to respond by bidding his longest and best suit. Usually a takeout double shows a good hand. A defender should not merely overcall if his hand is strong enough for a takeout double.

A double is for a takeout when:

1. The doubler's partner has not bid, doubled, or passed a double for penalties;

2. The double is made at the doubler's first opportunity;

3. The doubled bid is one, two or three in a suit.

The takeout doubled is most often used by the defenders but may be used also by the opener if his partner has not bid or doubled.

SOUTH	WEST	NORTH	EAST	SOUTH	WEST	NORTH	EAST
1 ♡	Double *(takeout)*			1 ♡	1 ♠	Pass	Pass
				Double *(takeout)*			

A player may repeat a takeout double if his partner did not respond to his first double or make a penalty pass.

SOUTH	WEST	NORTH	EAST	SOUTH	WEST	NORTH	EAST
1 ♡	Double 2 ♡	Pass		1 ♣	Double Pass		Pass
Pass	Double *(takeout)*			1 ♠	Double *(penalty)*		

Requirements

14 points or 3 quick tricks (usually more) with Support for every unbid suit, or
A strong rebiddable suit and support for one other suit

With strong support for every unbid suit, as with 4-4-4-1 distribution, a takeout double may be made on 11 to 13 points.

Examples, opponent having bid one diamond:

1. ♠ Q-J-6-3   ♡ 10-9-5-2   ◇ K-6   ♣ A-K-8   Double
2. ♠ A-6-5   ♡ K-Q-8-6-4   ◇ 2   ♣ A-7-4-3   Double
3. ♠ A-K-J-8-6-4   ♡ J-7-6-2   ◇ A   ♣ 4-3   Double
4. ♠ Q-6-3   ♡ A-J-7-5   ◇ 6   ♣ K-J-8-7-2   Double

When an opposing opening *suit-bid* is passed by the opener's partner, a takeout double to reopen the bidding may be shaded to 9 points.

Optional or Coöperative Doubles

A double of a preëmptive bid shows a strong hand but requires partner to bid only if he has a 5-card or longer suit. The double may be passed.

The doubler needs about 18 points to double a three-bid and about 16 points to double a four-bid, including support for the unbid suits.

See also the unusual notrump, page 70.

HOW TO TAKE OUT A DOUBLE

When your partner makes a takeout double of a suit-bid of one or two, and the next player passes, you must respond. *The weaker your hand, the greater the obligation to bid.*

A double of an opponent's preëmptive bid of three or four permits a pass (page 52) but it is better to bid unless the hand is weak and contains no long suit, or unless you have trump strength and expect to defeat the contract.

A double of an opening one-notrump bid should be passed except with a weak hand containing a 5-card or longer suit.

In responding, prefer a weak 5-card suit to a stronger 4-card suit unless the 4-card suit can be bid at a lower level.

WHEN THE DOUBLED BID IS IN A SUIT	IF YOU HOLD	WHEN THE DOUBLED BID IS NOTRUMP
BID your longest unbid suit. With suits of equal length, bid the one that can be shown at the lowest level. PASS only if there is an intervening bid or redouble.	Less than **5** pts.	BID a 5-card or longer suit. Lacking one, PASS. But take out in your best suit if an opponent redoubles.
BID your best suit (prefer a major) BID ONE NO-TRUMP with 7 or 8 points and an honor in opponents' suit PASS only with 4 trump tricks	**5** to **8** pts.	PASS for penalties. (But if *all* your strength is in one 5-card or longer suit, bid the suit. With 1½ tricks in a 6-card suit, jump to three.)
JUMP one trick in your best suit (prefer a major) or BID TWO NO-TRUMP with a double stopper in opponents' suit PASS only with 3 trump tricks.	**9** pts. or more	PASS. Only exception: Freak distribution which makes a game almost sure, in which case jump to three in a suit.

POINT-COUNT VALUATION

BIDDABLE SUITS

OPENING ONE-BIDS

CHOICE OF SUITS

FORCING BIDS

RESPONSES TO SUIT-BIDS

OPENER'S REBIDS

RESPONDER'S REBIDS

NOTRUMP BIDDING

OPENING 3, 4, 5 BIDS

FORCING TWO-BIDS

OVERCALLS

TAKEOUT DOUBLE

PENALTY DOUBLES

PART-SCORE

DUPLICATE

SLAM BIDS

4-5 NOTRUMP SLAM BIDS

BIDDING CONVENTIONS

PERCENTAGE TABLES

BIDDING SYSTEMS

OPENING LEADS

SIGNALS IN PLAY

COVERING HONORS

FINESSES

SAFETY PLAYS

END-PLAYS SQUEEZE

BRIDGE LAWS

GLOSSARY

OPTIONAL RESPONSES TO DOUBLES

The following are special responses to takeout doubles, used by many players.

Cue-bid Response to Takeout Double

In response to partner's takeout double, a bid in the doubled suit is itself a takeout bid, asking the doubler to bid his best suit. This response is in general use.

The doubler's partner should have at most two cards in the doubled suit, at least one 4-card major suit, and 8 or more high-card points.

SOUTH	WEST	NORTH	EAST	East may hold:	♠ J-7-3-2
1 ◊	Double	Pass	2 ◊		♡ 10-9-6-4
					◊ 6-3
					♣ A-K-5

Responsive Double

In response to partner's takeout double, if the opener's partner raises, a double is not for penalties but shows support for the unbid suits and requests the player who made the takeout double to select the suit.

The player who makes the responsive double shows 8 to 10 (or more) high-card points. Usually he is short in the doubled suit.

Some use the responsive double only when the opener's partner raised to two or three:

SOUTH	WEST	NORTH	EAST	East may hold:	♠ J-8-5-3
1 ◊	Double	2 ◊	Double		♡ K-10-5-2
		(or 3 ◊)			◊ 8-7
					♣ K-J-6

The responsive double may also be used when the opener's partner has bid a new suit at the level of one, two, or three. (If the opener's partner bids notrump, the double is for penalties.)

SOUTH	WEST	NORTH	EAST	East may hold:	♠ 8-7-3
1 ◊	Double	1 ♠	Double		♡ A-8-5-4
					◊ 6-5
					♣ K-Q-6-3

Notrump Response to Takeout Double

A response of 1 N T to partner's takeout double shows a fair hand (8 to 10 points) perhaps including only a partial stopper such as Q-x or J-x-x in the opponents' suit. A jump response of 2 N T shows 11 to 13 points including at least one sure stopper and usually a double stopper.

SOUTH	WEST	NORTH	EAST	East bids 1 N T:	East bids 2 N T:
1 ♠	Double	Pass	1 N T	♠ J-10-3	♠ K-J-6
		or		♡ J-5	♡ 7-2
SOUTH	WEST	NORTH	EAST	◊ A-8-5-4	◊ K-Q-8-7-4
1 ♠	Double	Pass	2 N T	♣ K-8-4-2	♣ Q-J-4

BIDS OVER AN OPPONENT'S DOUBLE

When an opponent makes a takeout double of partner's opening *suit-bid*, a bid by the responder is intended chiefly to make it difficult for the doubler's partner to respond.

If partner's bid was a preëmptive bid, raise with 3-card or longer trump support and fewer than 3 quick tricks.

If partner's bid was one of a suit:

REDOUBLE to show a strong hand—10 pts. or more.

RAISE to TWO with trump support and up to 6 pts.; to THREE with 4 or 5 trumps, a singleton, and 5 to 7 pts. (*Not forcing.*) Raise to FOUR if able (page 14).

BID ONE in a 5-card suit or TWO (if necessary) in a 6-card suit with 5 to 9 pts., if unable to raise. (*Not forcing.*)

PASS any hand, including a worthless hand or a hand of up to 9 pts., that does not fit the requirements for a redouble, raise, or bid.

Partner bids one heart. Opponent doubles.

1. ♠ 7-6   ♡ Q-7-4-2   ◇ K-8-5-4   ♣ 9-4-3   Two hearts
2. ♠ 7   ♡ Q-10-6-5   ◇ 10-9-6-5   ♣ K-J-4-3   Three hearts
3. ♠ A-10-5-3   ♡ 7-6   ◇ K-J-8-6   ♣ Q-7-6   Redouble
4. ♠ 10-9-2   ♡ —   ◇ K-8-2   ♣ A-K-Q-8-7-6-3   Three clubs

If partner's opening one-notrump bid is doubled:

REDOUBLE with 7 pts. or more.

BID a 6-card or longer suit in a weak hand (0 to 5 pts.).

BID a 5-card or longer suit with 4 to 6 pts.

JUMP to game in a major if you would do so over a pass.

PASS any other hand.

If Partner's Response is Doubled

If you have opened with a suit-bid of one; partner has responded; and the opponent on your right has made a takeout double:

REDOUBLE with 18 pts. or more.

RAISE partner's suit once, with adequate trump support but a minimum bid.

REBID a rebiddable suit, or bid a new biddable suit, with a singleton in partner's suit.

PASS with less.

Any bid warns that the hand is weak.

You are SOUTH
in this bidding:

	SOUTH	WEST	NORTH	EAST
	1 ◇	Pass	1 ♡	Double

South should now:

1. ♠ J-9-7-6   ♡ J-6   ◇ A-K-8-5   ♣ A-K-3   Redouble
2. ♠ Q-6-3   ♡ 2   ◇ A-Q-J-6-3-2   ♣ A-5-4   Two diamonds
3. ♠ 6-5   ♡ Q-7-2   ◇ A-Q-6-5   ♣ A-Q-5-4   Two hearts

PENALTY DOUBLES

A double is for *penalties* (to increase the value of undertrick penalties, in the expectation that the opposing contract will be defeated):

(a) Whenever the doubler's partner has made any bid, double or penalty pass.

(b) When the doubled bid is in notrump, or is four or more in a suit.

(c) When the doubler opened with a notrump bid or a bid of two or more in a suit, or

(d) In any event, if the doubler, at a previous opportunity to make a takeout double, did not do so.

When to Double for Penalties

When the opposing contract, if doubled and made, will produce a game, you should not double unless you can count enough probable *defensive winners* in the combined hands to defeat the opponents' contract *at least two tricks*, or enough *certain* winners to defeat it one trick. Avoid doubling slams.

The expected penalty must be worth more than any contract your side can *surely* bid and make.

How to Count Defensive Winners

Against the opponents' *trump* contract, count

1. *Honor-tricks at their defensive value only* (page 4). But in a suit bid by your left-hand opponent, K-x should not be counted at all, and A-Q should be expected to win only one trick.

2. *Honor-tricks in partner's hand* (as shown by his bidding).

3. *Trump tricks.* This includes any *stopper* in the opponent's suit (J-x-x-x, etc.). *Length* in the opponents' trump suit is more important than high cards.

Doubles of Notrump Bids

Usually a notrump bid should not be doubled unless the defenders probably have at least 20 points in high cards and also a strong suit to lead, such as Q-J-10-x, A-K-x-x-x, etc.

For example: ♠ A-7-3　♡ K-Q-5　♢ Q-6　♣ K-Q-J-7-2

When to Take Out a Penalty Double

Do not take out partner's penalty double *unless*

(a) The doubled bid is one notrump (page 53) or

(b) You have freak distribution (such as 5-5-3-0, 7-4-1-1, etc.) including a singleton or void in the opponents suit, *and* you expect to score more (or to lose less) by playing the hand. Partner's double of a 2 ♣ or 2 ♢ overcall should be taken out with a void or low singleton in the opponents' suit.

PART-SCORE BIDDING

A part-score by either side has an effect on bidding tactics. The side with the part-score should try to buy the contract at the lowest level sufficient for game; therefore this side should prefer bids, such as one notrump, that are most difficult for the opponents to overcall. The side that does not have the part-score should take extra chances to overcall and to "bid the opponents up" to a contract they may be unable to make.

WHEN YOU HAVE A PART-SCORE

1. A forcing two-bid, or a forcing takeout or forcing rebid (both of which are *jump* bids in a *new* suit), is still forcing, even though game has been reached. A bid in the opponents' suit is also forcing. After the first response to one of these forcing bids, a rebid in a *new* suit by *either partner* is again forcing for one round; but a rebid in notrump, or in a suit previously bid, may be passed.

2. Other bids that are usually forcing *may be passed* if a contract sufficient (with the part-score) for game has already been reached.

3. Keep partner's opening one-bid open with about 2 points *less,* or with *slightly* less trump support (such as 10-x-x) than is usually required. Thus, respond one notrump, or bid *one* in any biddable suit, with about 5 points.

4. Do not open the bidding *fourth hand* with the bare minimum requirements if your principal strength is in the minor suits.

5. An opening preëmptive bid (page 42), even though more than enough for game, is *not* a slam try.

WHEN YOUR OPPONENTS HAVE A PART-SCORE

1. Shade the requirements for opening bids to about 11 points and a rebiddable 4-card suit, as on such hands it would be even more dangerous to overcall later if an opponent opens the bidding.

2. Prefer to open the bidding with one notrump rather than a suit-bid with 4-4-3-2, 5-3-3-2 and even 6-3-2-2 hands.

3. Overcall an opponent's opening bid even with no high-card strength if you have enough *winners* (page 43).

DUPLICATE BRIDGE METHODS

Most duplicate bridge games are scored by match-points, and in such games your bidding methods should be modified as follows:

1. A vulnerable game made against you will give your opponents 600 to 660 points. You must therefore seek every possible sacrifice contract (page 41). In order to find your best combined trump suit most often, when you are not vulnerable and your opponents are vulnerable, overcall the opponents' opening bids with one winner less than you would require in rubber bridge. When you are not vulnerable, your overcalls and raises of partner's overcalls should be based on winners, regardless of high-card values.

2. Prefer to try for a probable vulnerable game rather than double nonvulnerable opponents for a sure 3-trick penalty.

3. Rather than make a doubtful overcall, reduce the requirements for takeout doubles by a few points when holding support for all unbid suits.

4. Do not fail to reopen the bidding (when an opening bid, or a weak response or rebid such as one notrump or two in a suit, is passed) if you have 8 or more points.

5. Seek major- rather than minor-suit contracts, and prefer to play notrump rather than suit slams in order to score the 10 points extra for tricks.

6. If you could make a part-score contract and the opponents overcall it, double them even when you expect to defeat them only one trick.

7. Avoid opening 3- or 4-bids when holding 2 or more honor-tricks. It may be possible to play the hand at a contract of two-odd or three-odd, respectively, and make it.

8. Whereas in rubber bridge you should try for a major-suit game with about 9 winners in the combined hands; and try for a small slam that depends on a successful finesse; stop short of these doubtful contracts in duplicate bridge.

9. Always consider first a double of an opponent's overcall or low contract, before making another bid, when your opponents are vulnerable and you are not. Beating them one trick (200 points) is better than any part-score contract you can make. Beating them two tricks (500 points) is better than any game you can make.

OPENING-BID SLAM TRIES

Opening bids of four or more in notrump, or five or six in a major suit, or six in a minor suit, carry special messages. The opener would have no purpose in bidding beyond game except as a slam try. These bids show specific strength and invite partner to raise to a slam only if he holds certain cards.

Notrump Bids Higher than Game

An opening bid of four, five or six notrump shows ability to win 10, 11 or 12 tricks, respectively, including:

> **28 or more points**
> **Ace or king in every suit**
> **4-3-3-3 distribution**

The notrump slam try is now seldom used in expert circles, its place having been taken by the two-club bid (page 44).

Responses to High Notrump Bids

Responses to high opening notrump bids are based on the fact that when the opening hand contains so many honor-tricks, any Queen or higher card in the responding hand is a full trick. Therefore, in raising:

Raise an opening four-notrump bid to six with two cards, Queen or higher; to seven with three such cards.
Raise an opening five-notrump bid to six with one Queen, and to seven with two Queens (or higher).
Raise an opening six-notrump bid with one Queen or higher card.

Any 5-card suit is probably worth two tricks opposite such a hand, *since partner guarantees at least three cards in support*. Bid a 5-card suit headed by a Queen or higher, or any 6-card suit. Over four notrump jump to six in a 5-card suit headed by a Queen.

Suit-bids of Five or Six

An opening bid of five in a major suit, and of six in a major or minor suit, guarantees as many sure winners as the amount of the bid, and shows a hand with no losers except in the trump suit.

Raise such a bid once for each trump honor as high as the Queen; do not raise on outside strength, no matter how great.

Examples of opening bids that are slam tries:
1. ♠ A-K-6	♡ K-Q-J-10	◇ A-K-Q	♣ A-Q-J	Four notrump
2. ♠ A-K-Q	♡ A-K-Q	◇ A-K-6-5	♣ A-K-8	Four notrump
3. ♠ A-K-Q	♡ A-K-Q	◇ A-K-J-10	♣ A-K-7	Five notrump
4. ♠ Q-J-10-9-8-7-5	♡ A-K-Q-J	◇ A-K	♣ —	Five spades
5. ♠ A	♡ —	◇ —	♣ K-Q-J-10-9-8-7-6-5-4-3-2	Six clubs

Response, if partner opens four notrump:
1. ♠ Q-8-7-4-3	♡ 6-3	◇ 7-4-2	♣ 8-6-2	Five spades
2. ♠ Q-4	♡ A-6-2	◇ 9-6-3-2	♣ 8-6-5-2	Six notrump

Response, if partner opens five spades:
1. ♠ K	♡ 7-6-3-2	◇ 8-7-5-3	♣ 6-5-4-2	Six spades
2. ♠ 6-5-3-2	♡ A	◇ Q-10-6	♣ A-K-Q-J-7	Pass

POINT-COUNT VALUATION

BIDDABLE SUITS

OPENING ONE-BIDS

CHOICE OF SUITS

FORCING BIDS

RESPONSES TO SUIT-BIDS

OPENER'S REBIDS

RESPONDER'S REBIDS

NOTRUMP BIDDING

OPENING 3, 4, 5 BIDS

FORCING TWO-BIDS

OVERCALLS

TAKEOUT DOUBLE

PENALTY DOUBLES

PART-SCORE

DUPLICATE

SLAM BIDS

4-5 NOTRUMP SLAM BIDS

BIDDING CONVENTIONS

PERCENTAGE TABLES

BIDDING SYSTEMS

OPENING LEADS

SIGNALS IN PLAY

COVERING HONORS

FINESSES

SAFETY PLAYS

END-PLAYS SQUEEZE

BRIDGE LAWS

GLOSSARY

WHEN TO TRY FOR A SLAM

When you are sure that you and your partner together have 31 points or more, you *may* be in the slam zone. Before bidding a slam, you should check on the following.

HIGH CARDS

Except with freak hands, 33 high-card points are usually needed to make a small slam, especially at notrump. The opponents then will have at most 7 pts., perhaps an ace and a king, in which case a finesse may be needed to make the slam. A grand slam usually requires 37 pts. or freakish distribution. The combined high-card count is inferred by adding your own count to the minimum promised by partner's bidding.

THE TRUMP AND SIDE SUITS

At least eight trumps in the combined hands, including at least three of the four top honors (A, K and Q; or A, Q and J; or K, Q and J). In addition to the trump suit, there must usually be a strong, 5-card or longer *side suit* in the hand of one partner.

TOP CONTROLS IN SUITS

First-round control is a card which will win a trick the first time its suit is led. An ace, or a void suit at trump contracts, is first-round control.

Second-round control is the ability to win the second lead of a suit, after the opponents have won the first lead with the ace. Any king, or at trump contracts a singleton, is second-round control.

Every slam depends on controls. With the necessary controls, a small slam may be made with as few as 28 high-card points (even less in freakish cases). Lacking controls, one may be unable to make a slam with 33 or even 34 high-card points. In the case of the king as a second-round control, all may depend on who becomes declarer. If the king is in dummy, the opening lead may cause two immediate tricks to be lost to an opponent's A-Q.

For a small slam you must have first-round control in three suits and at least second-round control in the fourth suit. For a grand slam you need first-round control in all four suits; a *solid* combined trump suit; and 13 sure winners.

When you can assume the combined hands to fulfill all these requirements, you may make a slam try or bid.

60

DIRECT SLAM TRIES

The Blackwood and other slam conventions (page 63) are used in expert games chiefly when the combined strength of the partners' hands is known and there is necessity only to make sure that the necessary controls are present. On this and the next page are given direct slam tries, which precede or replace the conventional slam tries.

On this page and page 62, *cue-bid* designates a control-showing bid for slam purposes. The term has other applications—see pages 75 and 77.

A Bid of More than Game

An *unnecessary* bid of more than game is a slam invitation (except in some *part-score* situations).

SOUTH	WEST	NORTH	EAST
1 ♠	Pass	2 ♣	Pass
4 ♠	Pass	5 ♣	

Unnecessary bid of more than game—slam try.

SOUTH	WEST	NORTH	EAST
1 ♠	2 ◇	4 ♠	5 ◇
Pass	Pass	5 ♠	

Not a slam try, because necessary to overcall opponents.

MAKE a slam invitation when all the slam requirements (see opposite page) are *probably* present.

ACCEPT your partner's slam invitation when you have *any* strength (even a plus value, or extra length or strength in the trump suit) which has not been fully disclosed by your previous bids.

However, the partner who has made the stronger bids should generally not make or accept a slam try without at least two aces.

SOUTH	WEST	NORTH	EAST
1 ♠	Pass	2 ◇	Pass
3 ♠	Pass	5 ♠	

North's five-spade bid is a slam invitation. He may hold
♠ Q-7-2 ♡ K-Q-8-4 ♣ J-7-5-3

South's three-spade bid promised a 6-card suit and (usually) at least 19 points. South's action now should be:

♠ A-K-9-6-4-3 ♡ K-Q-6 ◇ 7-5 ♣ K-Q Pass—only one Ace
♠ A-K-10-6-4-3-2 ♡ A-Q-6 ◇ J-3 ♣ 8 Six spades

Control-showing Bids (Cue-bids)

A bid in the opponents' suit is a slam try. It guarantees first-round control (ace or void) of that suit, plus very strong support for partner's suit (or a solid trump suit in the bidder's own hand).

SOUTH	WEST	NORTH	EAST
1 ♡	1 ♠	2 ♠	

North has first-round spade control and powerful heart support. *South should respond as to a forcing takeout* (page 27). If South is strong in the spade suit, he should bid no-trump.

SOUTH	WEST	NORTH	EAST
1 ♡	1 ♠	2 ◇	Pass
2 ♠			

South has first-round spade control and either powerful diamond support or a powerful heart suit. South's bid is forcing to game and North must bid again.

POINT-COUNT VALUATION

BIDDABLE SUITS

OPENING ONE-BIDS

CHOICE OF SUITS

FORCING BIDS

RESPONSES TO SUIT-BIDS

OPENER'S REBIDS

RESPONDER'S REBIDS

NOTRUMP BIDDING

OPENING 3, 4, 5 BIDS

FORCING TWO-BIDS

OVERCALLS

TAKEOUT DOUBLE

PENALTY DOUBLES

PART-SCORE

DUPLICATE

SLAM BIDS

4-5 NOTRUMP SLAM BIDS

BIDDING CONVENTIONS

PERCENTAGE TABLES

BIDDING SYSTEMS

OPENING LEADS

SIGNALS IN PLAY

COVERING HONORS

FINESSES

SAFETY PLAYS

END-PLAYS SQUEEZE

BRIDGE LAWS

GLOSSARY

DIRECT SLAM TRIES (Cont'd)
Cue-bids

A cue-bid is a bid to show control of a suit that will not be the trump suit. Usually it is a bid in a new suit, after some trump suit has been agreed upon, and usually it is a slam try. Always it is a bid not necessary to reach game.

South	West	North	East		South	West	North	East
1 ◇	Pass	1 ♡	Pass		1 ◇	Pass	1 ♠	Pass
3 ♡	Pass	4 ♣ *Cue-bid*			3 ♡	Pass	4 ◇ *Cue-bid*	

In each case a satisfactory trump suit has been found, so North's only purpose can have been to give information leading to a slam. North shows control of the suit he bids. In the first example it must be the ace, in the second at least the king.

A cue-bid may be made before the trump suit is agreed upon, if a later bid makes the situation clear.

South	West	North	East		South	West	North	East
1 ♠	Pass	2 ♡	Pass		1 ◇	Pass	1 ♠	Pass
3 ♠	Pass	3 ◇	Pass		2 ♡	Pass	3 ♠	Pass
4 ♡					4 ♣ *Cue-bid*			

Obviously South could have raised hearts earlier; therefore his three-club bid was a cue-bid. | Each partner has shown strength. If South has clubs and wished only a game, he could have bid three no-trump.

A cue-bid invites another cue-bid, usually at the lowest possible level. A bid in a suit in which partner has made a cue-bid shows at least the king of that suit.

South	West	North	East		South	West	North	East
1 ♣	Pass	3 ♠	Pass		1 ◇	Pass	2 ♡	Pass
4 ♣	Pass	4 ♡			3 ♡	Pass	4 ♣	Pass
					5 ♣			

North accepts the slam try, shows the heart ace, and denies the diamond ace. | South shows the king of clubs, or perhaps a void or singleton.

A void suit may be cue-bid, but only when the partnership has established fits in two suits.

South	West	North	East		South	West	North	East
1 ♡	Pass	2 ♣	Pass		1 ♡	Pass	2 ♣	Pass
2 ♠	Pass	3 ◇			3 ♠	Pass	4 ♡	Pass
					5 ♣	Pass	5 ◇	

The three-diamond bid should not be a cue-bid showing a void. | Five diamonds is a cue-bid, perhaps a void.

Double of a Cue-bid

A double of an opponent's cue-bid (or a double of an artificial response, as to a Blackwood 4 N T) is used to direct partner's opening lead when the opponents seem to be on their way to a slam.

South	West	North	East
1 ◇	Pass	2 ♡	Pass
3 ♡	Pass	4 ♣	Pass
5 ♣	Double		

North is likely to play a six-heart slam and East will have the opening lead. West's double tells East to open a club.

The doubler should have at least K-Q (or Ace) plus length in the doubled suit—for example, K-Q-10-x-x.

4- AND 5-NOTRUMP SLAM TRIES

Bids of four and five notrump are used as slam tries, since each represents a contract at which one would not voluntarily play. The principal example, almost universally used, is the Blackwood Convention.*

The Blackwood Convention

When either partner has bid a suit, and when the previous bidding has not precluded the possibility of a slam, a bid of four notrump is forcing and requires partner to respond as follows:

Five clubs, if he has *no* ace or *all four* aces.
Five diamonds, if he has *one* ace.
Five hearts, if he has *two* aces.
Five spades, if he has *three* aces.

[Originally, a 5 N T response was used to show all four Aces and the 5 ♣ response was used only to deny holding any ace. *Many players still use the 5 N T response.* But the previous bidding will always tell whether the responder can have an aceless hand or must have all four aces.]

If, after one of these responses, the four-notrump bidder bids *five* notrump, he shows that he has located all four aces and he requires his partner to show the number of his kings on a similar schedule.

Six clubs, if he has *no* king.
Six diamonds, if he has *one* king.
Six hearts, if he has *two* kings.
Six spades, if has has *three* kings.
Six notrump, if he has *all four* kings.

The player who bids the Blackwood 4 N T is in charge. He designates the final contract.

When Four Notrump is Not Forcing

A bid of four notrump is not conventional and is not forcing, in the following cases:

South	West	North	East
1 ♡	2 ◇	2 N T	Pass
3 N T	Pass	Pass	4 ◇
Pass	Pass	4 N T	

Not forcing; if North had wanted a slam he would not have passed before.

South	West	North	East
1 ♡	4 ♠	Pass	Pass
4 N T			

Not forcing. South opened with a one-bid; North passed. South cannot be making a slam try.

South	West	North	East
4 ♠	4 N T		

Forcing, but not for ace-showing. East-West have bid no suit. East is expected to respond in his best suit.

South	West	North	East
1 ♡	Pass	3 N T	Pass
4 N T	(not forcing)		

A direct raise of a jump bid in notrump is a slam try but not a conventional bid.

*Devised in 1933 by Easley Blackwood. Ely Culbertson had introduced his 4-5 N T Convention (page 65) that year, and Blackwood's convention soon superseded the original.

POINT-COUNT VALUATION

BIDDABLE SUITS

OPENING ONE-BIDS

CHOICE OF SUITS

FORCING BIDS

RESPONSES TO SUIT-BIDS

OPENER'S REBIDS

RESPONDER'S REBIDS

NOTRUMP BIDDING

OPENING 3, 4, 5 BIDS

FORCING TWO-BIDS

OVERCALLS

TAKEOUT DOUBLE

PENALTY DOUBLES

PART-SCORE

DUPLICATE

SLAM BIDS

4-5 NOTRUMP SLAM BIDS

BIDDING CONVENTIONS

PERCENTAGE TABLES

BIDDING SYSTEMS

OPENING LEADS

SIGNALS IN PLAY

COVERING HONORS

FINESSES

SAFETY PLAYS

END-PLAYS SQUEEZE

BRIDGE LAWS

GLOSSARY

4- AND 5-NOTRUMP SLAM TRIES
The Blackwood Convention (Continued)

If the four-notrump bidder wishes to play at five notrump (as in a tournament), he bids five of an unbid suit and his partner must bid five notrump.

SOUTH	WEST	NORTH	EAST	
1 ♠	Pass	2 ◇	Pass	North's five-diamond response showed one ace, which
3 N T	Pass	4 ◇	Pass	South deemed insufficient for
4 N T	Pass	5 ◇	Pass	a slam. South will pass five
5 ♡	Pass	5 N T	Pass	notrump.

When an opponent overcalls the four-notrump bid, the responder may double for penalties or may respond by starting at the level of the overcall and responding one level higher for each ace he holds.

SOUTH	WEST	NORTH	EAST	
1 ♣	1 ♡	3 ♣	3 ♡	North will respond: Pass if he has no ace, five spades with
4 ♣	Pass	4 ◇	Pass	one ace, five notrump with
4 N T	5 ♡			two aces, etc.

If the responder wishes to show a void, he skips one step. Over four notrump he bids:

With one ace and a void **Six diamonds**
With two aces and a void **Six hearts**
With three aces and a void **Six spades**

If the bid required to show the aces and the void is at a higher level than the agreed trump suit, the responder shows his aces but not his void.

When Not to Use Blackwood

The Blackwood Convention should not be used: 1. When a trump fit has not been found. 2. When there is no safe contract over an unfavorable response. 3. When the bidder cannot profit from knowing how many aces his partner has.

SOUTH	WEST	NORTH	EAST	South holds:
1 ♡	Pass	3 ◇	Pass	♠ A-7-3
3 N T	Pass	4 ♣	Pass	♡ K-J-8-5-4
				◇ K-J
				♣ Q-J-3

South should not bid four notrump. He does not know where to play the hand.

SOUTH	WEST	NORTH	EAST	South holds: ♠ A-Q-3
1 ♣	Pass	1 ◇	Pass	♡ 7
3 ♣	Pass	4 ♣	Pass	◇ K-J-2
				♣ K-Q-J-10-9-6

South should not bid four notrump. If North responds five diamonds, showing one ace, South cannot bid six but cannot safely pass.

SOUTH	WEST	NORTH	EAST	North holds: ♠ A-4
1 ♣	Pass	3 ♡	Pass	♡ A-K-8-6-3-2
4 ♣	Pass			◇ A-J-6
				♣ 6-3

North should not bid four notrump. Even if South shows one ace and three kings, North cannot safely bid seven. North should bid four diamonds to let South bid four notrump. If South has ♠ K-Q-J-6-3 ♡ Q-J ◇ K-5 ♣ A-K-8-4, South can bid four and five notrump and then safely bid seven notrump.

4- AND 5-NOTRUMP SLAM TRIES
Roman Blackwood

This method of responding to four notrump is used in the Roman Club System (page 65) but may be incorporated into any system. Responses are:

    5 ♣—no ace or 3 aces
    5 ◇—1 ace or 4 aces
    5 ♡—2 aces, both red, both black, both major, or both minor
    5 ♠—2 aces, not matched (♠ & ◇ or ♡ & ♣)

King-showing, over a five-notrump bid, is on the same basis but one level higher.

San Francisco Responses

Each ace is counted as 3 pts., each king 1 pt.

<table>
<tr><th colspan="3">RESPONSE</th></tr>
<tr><th>IF OPENING BID
WAS A ONE-BID</th><th></th><th>IF OPENING BID WAS
A TWO-BID OR 2 N T</th></tr>
<tr><td>No ace</td><td>5 ♣</td><td>No ace or king</td></tr>
<tr><td>3 pts. (A or K-K-K)</td><td>5 ◇</td><td>1 pt. (1 king)</td></tr>
<tr><td>4 pts. (A + K or 4 K's)</td><td>5 ♡</td><td>2 pts. (K-K)</td></tr>
<tr><td>5 pts. (A + K-K)</td><td>5 ♠</td><td>3 pts. (A or K-K-K)</td></tr>
<tr><td>6 pts. (A-A or A-K-K-K)</td><td>5 N T</td><td>4 pts. (A + K or 4 K's)</td></tr>
<tr><td>7 pts. (A-A-K or A & 4 K's)</td><td>6 ♣</td><td>5 pts. (A + K-K)</td></tr>
<tr><td>8 pts. (A-A + K-K)</td><td>6 ◇</td><td>6 pts. (A-A or A-K-K-K)</td></tr>
</table>

And one step higher for each additional point.

Culbertson 4-5 Notrump Convention

This, the original ace-showing convention, is still used in Acol and other European systems. The four-notrump bidder shows controls as well as asking about them; therefore either partner may make the final decision about the contract.

Subject to the exceptions on page 63, a bid of four notrump is forcing and shows

    Any three aces; or
    Two aces plus the king of "a bid suit" (a suit previously bid by the bidder or his partner).

Partner must respond as follows, holding:

    TWO ACES, or **ONE ACE** and the kings of all bid suits—5 N T.
    ONE ACE or a **VOID** in an unbid suit—bid five in the suit.
    ONE ACE in a bid suit, or **NO ACE** but the kings of all bid suits—jump to six in the best available trump suit.
    LESS than the above requirements—SIGN OFF by bidding five in the *lowest* suit previously bid by either partner. This does *not* indicate support for that suit.

When the player who bids four notrump rebids five notrump, he (or his side) has all four aces.

GERBER CONVENTION

The Gerber Convention* is a variation of the Blackwood Convention designed to permit ace-showing below the game level. The rules are:

A four-club bid is conventional and forcing, requiring partner to show the number of his aces by responding as follows.

> 4 ◇ if he has no ace
> 4 ♡ if he has one ace
> 4 ♠ if he has two aces
> 4 N T if he has three aces
> 5 ♣ if he has four aces (but many users adopt the Blackwood principle and let 4 ◇ show either no ace or all four aces)

The Gerber four-club slam try is widely used, but only when

> The four-club bid is a jump bid;
> The opening bid was in notrump; or
> The bid preceding the four-club bid was in notrump.

South	West	North	East
1 N T	Pass	4 ♣ (Gerber)	

South	West	North	East
1 ♠	Pass	2 N T	Pass
4 ♣ (Gerber)			

South	West	North	East
1 N T	Pass	3 ♡	Pass
3 N T	Pass	4 ♣ (not Gerber)	

South	West	North	East
2 N T	Pass	3 ♣	Pass
3 ♡	Pass	4 ♣ (not Gerber)	

Gerber King-Showing

When the Gerber Convention is used in all bidding situations, not only in notrump bidding, kings may be shown after the original four-club bid and response.

If the four-club bidder bids the next-higher denomination over his partner's response, he asks for a showing of kings on the same step system:

> **One step higher—no king**
> **Two steps higher—one king**
> **Three steps higher—two kings**
> etc.

South	West	North	East	
1 ♡	Pass	3 ♡	Pass	In response to South's 4 ♣,
4 ♣	Pass	4 ♡	Pass	North showed one ace. Now
4 ♠	Pass	5 ◇		4 ♠ asked for kings and

North showed two kings.

Many play that only a five-club rebid, following the Gerber four-club bid and the response to it, asks for kings. Other rebids by the four-club bidder are natural. Responses to five clubs are the same as to four clubs but one level higher.

*Introduced by John Gerber of Houston.

THE GRAND SLAM FORCE

This convention* is used after a trump suit has been unmistakably agreed upon.

If then a player makes a free five-notrump bid, he demands that his partner bid seven in the agreed trump suit holding two of the three top honors (K-Q, A-Q, or A-K) in that suit.

SOUTH	WEST	NORTH	EAST	South holds:	♠ Q-J-6-4-3
1 ♠	Pass	2 ♣	Pass		♡ A-K-6-3
3 ♡	Pass	4 ♠	Pass		◇ A-K-7-2
5 N T	Pass				♣ —

South wishes to play at seven spades if North has ♠ A-K and at six spades if North has any other spade holding consistent with North's bidding.

In response to the grand slam force, the partner must bid seven if he has the required cards and must bid six (in the agreed trump suit) if he lacks the exact top cards that his partner asks for. He is not permitted to exercise judgment.

The grand slam force may be used by either partner.

If no suit has been agreed upon, a jump to five notrump sets the last bid suit as the trump suit.

SOUTH	WEST	NORTH	EAST	North holds:	♠ K-J-6
1 ♠	Pass	3 ♣	Pass		♡ A-8-5
3 ♠	Pass	5 N T			◇ —
					♣ A-K-9-8-6-5-3

Spades are the agreed trump suit. North can expect a grand slam to be made if South has at least ♠ A-Q-x-x-x.

The grand slam force need not be a jump bid, when a suit has been agreed upon and both partners have shown strength.

SOUTH	WEST	NORTH	EAST	North holds:	♠ 2
1 ♠	Pass	2 ◇	Pass		♡ A-4
3 ♡	Pass	4 ◇	Pass		◇ A-J-8-6-4-3
5 ◇	Pass	5 N T			♣ A-8-5-3

Other responses may supply information as valuable toward reaching a grand slam as the direct seven-bid.

If the agreed suit is spades, responder may bid six hearts with ♠ A-x-x-x-x or ♠ K-x-x-x-x; six diamonds with ♠ A-x-x-x or ♠ K-x-x-x; six clubs with ♠ x-x-x-x-x.

If the agreed suit is hearts, responder may bid six diamonds with ♡ A-x-x-x-x or ♡ K-x-x-x-x; six clubs with ♡ A-x-x-x or ♡ K-x-x-x.

If the agreed suit is diamonds, responder may bid six clubs with ◇ A-x-x-x-x or ◇ K-x-x-x-x.

Lacking these requirements, the responder signs off at six of the agreed trump suit.

*Original with Ely Culbertson in 1936.

POINT-COUNT VALUATION

BIDDABLE SUITS

OPENING ONE-BIDS

CHOICE OF SUITS

FORCING BIDS

RESPONSES TO SUIT-BIDS

OPENER'S REBIDS

RESPONDER'S REBIDS

NOTRUMP BIDDING

OPENING 3, 4, 5 BIDS

FORCING TWO-BIDS

OVERCALLS

TAKEOUT DOUBLE

PENALTY DOUBLES

PART-SCORE

DUPLICATE

SLAM BIDS

4-5 NOTRUMP SLAM BIDS

BIDDING CONVENTIONS

PERCENTAGE TABLES

BIDDING SYSTEMS

OPENING LEADS

SIGNALS IN PLAY

COVERING HONORS

FINESSES

SAFETY PLAYS

END-PLAYS SQUEEZE

BRIDGE LAWS

GLOSSARY

ASKING BIDS

Asking bids, introduced by Ely Culbertson in 1936, are a slam-bidding convention used to locate second-round controls. Asking bids proved too difficult for the average player in the United States but have remained popular abroad.

A player's hand may be strong enough for a slam, except that he has a weak suit in which his opponents may win the two tricks they need to stop a slam. To find out whether or not his partner can control this suit, the player may use an artificial, forcing bid known as an ASKING BID. The suit in which he makes the asking bid is the suit he wants to find out about.

The Agreed Trump Suit

An asking bid may not be made until the partners have agreed upon a trump suit in which to play the hand.

If a suit has been bid by one partner and raised by the other partner, that is the agreed trump suit.

If two suits have been bid and raised, the last raised suit is the agreed trump suit.

HOW TO RECOGNIZE AN ASKING BID

When a suit has previously been bid and raised, thus becoming the agreed trump suit,

Any bid in a new suit (not previously bid by either partner), if made at the level of four or higher, is an asking bid.

It does not mean that the bidder has any strength in that suit, or is willing to play the hand in that suit. Its sole effect is to ask partner what he holds in the specific asked suit.

1.	SOUTH	NORTH
	1 ♠	3 ♠
	4 ♣ (Asking Bid)	
	Trump Suit: Spades	

2.	SOUTH	NORTH
	1 ♠	2 ♠
	4 ♣ (Asking Bid)	
	Trump Suit: Spades	

3.	SOUTH	NORTH
	1 ♡	1 ♠
	3 ♠	4 ♡

Four hearts is NOT an asking bid. An asking bid must be made in a suit not previously bid by either partner.

4.	SOUTH	NORTH
	1 ♡	1 ♠
	3 ♠	4 ♣

Four clubs is an asking bid. Either partner may make an asking bid, no matter which one opened the bidding.
Trump suit: Spades.

After an asking bid, the asker's partner must sign off unless he holds at least second-round control (King, singleton, or better) in the asked suit. If not forced to sign off, he responds in such a way as to give as much information as possible about his hand. Responses to asking bids are given on the next page.

RESPONSES TO ASKING BIDS

Most asking bids are four-bids, although sometimes an asking bid is made at the level of five or even six. In illustrating the responses to asking bids, we will assume the following bidding:

SOUTH	WEST	NORTH	EAST
1 ♠	Pass	3 ♠	Pass
4 ♣ (Asking Bid)			

The *asked suit* is clubs; the *agreed trump suit* is spades.

HOLDING	NORTH'S RESPONSE
Neither first- nor second-round control in the asked suit	Sign off by bidding the agreed trump suit at the lowest possible level ♠ A-Q-6-3 ♡ A-K ◇ Q-J-8-2 ♣ 9-7-5-4 = Four spades
Second-round control in the asked suit but no Ace	Sign off as above ♠ K-Q-8-5 ♡ K-Q-J ◇ 10-9-5-4-3 ♣ 9 = Four spades
King or singleton in asked suit, Ace in agreed suit	Jump one trick in the agreed suit (so it will not be confused with a sign-off) ♠ A-Q-8-5 ♡ K-Q-J ◇ 10-9-5-4-3 ♣ 9 = Five spades
King or singleton in asked suit, one outside Ace	Bid the suit in which the Ace is held ♠ K-Q-8-5 ♡ A-K-6 ◇ 10-9-5-1-3 ♣ 9 = Four hearts
Ace in asked suit, no outside Ace	Raise the asked suit. Bid five clubs: ♠ K-Q-8-5 ♡ K-Q-6 ◇ 9-7 ♣ A-8-4-3
King or singleton in asked suit, two outside Aces	Four notrump ♠ A-Q-8-5 ♡ A-6-4-3 ◇ 8-5 ♣ K-J-7
Ace in asked suit, one outside Ace	Four notrump ♠ A-Q-8-5 ♡ K-Q-6 ◇ 8-5 ♣ A-8-4-3
First- or second-round control, with three Aces	Five notrump ♠ A-Q-8-5 ♡ A-7-6 ◇ 8-5 ♣ A-8-4-3 ♠ A-Q-8-5 ♡ A-7-6-4 ◇ A-9-7-3 ♣ 9

Choice of Ace or Void in Responding

1. When the responding hand contains a void, *but no Ace*, treat the void suit as though it were an Ace.

2. When the responding hand contains a void *and* an Ace in side suits, together with second-round control of the asked suit, show the Ace. Disregard the void.

3. With Ace in the asked suit, and a void outside, *show the void*. With void in the asked suit, Ace outside, *show the Ace*.

♠ K-Q-8-5-2 ♡ — ◇ K-Q-6-3 ♣ K-7-5-4   Four hearts
♠ K-Q-8-5-2 ♡ K-7-5-4 ◇ K-Q-6-3 ♣ —   Five clubs
♠ K-Q-8-5-2 ♡ — ◇ K-J-6-3 ♣ A-8-4-3   Four hearts
♠ K-Q-8-5-2 ♡ A-8-4-3 ◇ K-J-4-3 ♣ —   Four hearts

POINT-COUNT VALUATION

BIDDABLE SUITS

OPENING ONE-BIDS

CHOICE OF SUITS

FORCING BIDS

RESPONSES TO SUIT-BIDS

OPENER'S REBIDS

RESPONDER'S REBIDS

NOTRUMP BIDDING

OPENING 3, 4, 5 BIDS

FORCING TWO-BIDS

OVERCALLS

TAKEOUT DOUBLE

PENALTY DOUBLES

PART-SCORE

DUPLICATE

SLAM BIDS

4-5 NOTRUMP SLAM BIDS

BIDDING CONVENTIONS

PERCENTAGE TABLES

BIDDING SYSTEMS

OPENING LEADS

SIGNALS IN PLAY

COVERING HONORS

FINESSES

SAFETY PLAYS

END-PLAYS SQUEEZE

BRIDGE LAWS

GLOSSARY

THE UNUSUAL NOTRUMP

This convention, originally a part of the Roth-Stone System (page 88), has been widely adopted. In its simplest form it is a competitive notrump bid at the two-, three-, or occasionally four-level by a player who cannot have a hand strong enough to play such a contract. It usually shows a hand with great length in diamonds and clubs, and forces partner to bid the better of his minor suits, even if he holds only two or three cards in that suit.

When the opponents are bidding a major suit or suits, any notrump bid by a passed hand is "unusual" and asks for a minor-suit preference from partner. The assumption is that he cannot wish to play a notrump contract if he was too weak to open the bidding. The notrump bidder need not have any defensive tricks but should have at least ten cards in the minor suits, usually divided 5-5 but occasionally 6-4.

South	West	North	East
Pass	Pass	1 ♠	Pass
1 N T	Pass	2 ♠	Pass
Pass	2 N T	Pass	

South	West	North	East
1 ♡	Pass	1 ♠	Pass
2 ♣	2 N T	Pass	

West has: *East bids 3 ◊:*
- ♠ 5-4
- ♡ 3
- ◊ K-J-10-6-2
- ♣ A-Q-7-4-3

- ♠ 9-6-3
- ♡ K-J-8-5-4
- ◊ 8-7-3
- ♣ K-5

West has: *East bids 3 ♣:*
- ♠ 7
- ♡ 8-2
- ◊ Q-J-10-8-3
- ♣ K-Q-7-6-2

- ♠ 7-5-2
- ♡ Q-8-4-3
- ◊ 9-7-6
- ♣ A-10-4

When the notrump bidder puts in his bid at the one-level, after passing, he needs less high-card strength than he would need at the two-level. If the notrump bidder has not previously passed, he shows the unusual nature of his notrump bid by jumping. With the values for a genuine 2 N T bid, he would double first, then bid notrump.

South	West	North	East
Pass	1 ♡	Pass	1 ♠
1 N T			

South has: ♠ 6
♡ 4-2
◊ A-10-9-6-3
♣ Q-J-5-4-2

South	West	North	East
1 ♣	2 N T		

(Not used by all players)

West has: ♠ 2
♡ J-5
◊ A-Q-J-9-3
♣ K-Q-9-7-6

When the opponents have shown strength in two suits, one major and one minor, the unusual notrump is used to show a two-suiter in the unbid suits. Partner's response will be in the unbid suit in which he is longer.

South	West	North	East
Pass	1 ♠	Pass	2 ◊
2 N T (hearts and clubs)			

This application of the unusual notrump is not accepted by all players.

POINT-COUNT
VALUATION

BIDDABLE
SUITS

OPENING
ONE-BIDS

CHOICE
OF SUITS

FORCING BIDS

RESPONSES
TO SUIT-BIDS

OPENER'S
REBIDS

RESPONDER'S
REBIDS

NOTRUMP
BIDDING

OPENING
3, 4, 5 BIDS

FORCING
TWO-BIDS

OVERCALLS

TAKEOUT
DOUBLE

PENALTY
DOUBLES

PART-SCORE

DUPLICATE

SLAM BIDS

4-5 NOTRUMP
SLAM BIDS

BIDDING
CONVENTIONS

PERCENTAGE
TABLES

BIDDING
SYSTEMS

OPENING
LEADS

SIGNALS
IN PLAY

COVERING
HONORS

FINESSES

SAFETY PLAYS

END-PLAYS
SQUEEZE

BRIDGE LAWS

GLOSSARY

THE UNUSUAL NOTRUMP (Cont'd)
Responses on Strong Hands

Since his response is forced and he may have to bid a worthless hand, the notrump bidder's partner should make a free response or a jump response with a fair hand (8 pts. or so) that fits his partner's two-suiter; but in the opponents' suits only aces are likely to be valuable.

South	West	North	East		South	West	North	East
1 ♠	Pass	2 ♦	Pass		1 ♦	Pass	1 ♠	Pass
2 ♠	2 N T	4 ♠	5 ♣		2 ♦	2 N T	Pass	4 ♡

West has:	*East has:*	*West has:*	*East has:*
♠ 5	♠ 7-3-2	♠ 5	♠ 7-3-2
♡ A-8-6-4-3-2	♡ K-7	♡ Q-J-10-6-3	♡ A-7-5-4
♦ 9	♦ A-5-3	♦ 8	♦ 10-9-6-3
♣ K-10-7-4-3	♣ Q-9-6-5-2	♣ Q-J-10-7-5-4	♣ K-6

The Unusual Notrump at High Levels

When the opponents are vulnerable, the unusual notrump may be used at a high level as a preëmptive bid, to prepare for a sacrifice and at the same time crowd the bidding.

South	West	North	East		*West has:* ♠ —
1 ♠	4 N T				♡ 4
N-S vulnerable.					♦ Q-J-10-8-5-4
					♣ K-Q-J-6-3-2

When the opponents have reached a game or slam, the unusual notrump may be used at any level to reach a sacrifice contract.

South	West	North	East		*East has:* ♠ 10-9-7-6-3-2
2 ♦	Pass	3 ♣	Pass		♡ Q-J-9-7-5-2
3 ♦	ass	4 ♣	Pass		♦ —
4 N T	Pass	5 ♦	Pass		♣ 10
5 N T	Pass	6 ♦	6NT		
7 ♦	7 ♡	Double			

A grand slam in diamonds would be worth 2,140 points to North-South. Six notrump asked West to sacrifice in spades or hearts. At seven hearts West is down five for a 900-point loss, saving 1,240 points.

When a Notrump Overcall is Not Unusual

Care must be taken to avoid the misunderstandings that frequently arise when the notrump bidder intends his notrump overcall to be read as genuine and his partner construes it as unusual. It is probably safest to require any notrump overcall to be genuine unless the notrump-bidder passed at a previous turn.

South	West	North	East		South	West	North	East
1 ♡	Pass	2 ♡	2NT		1 ♣	1 ♡	Pass	2 ♡
					2 N T			

Genuine notrump bid—West should raise to 3 N T with about 6 points in high cards.

Genuine notrump bid. North may raise with about 6 points.

The notrump bid in each case shows a desire to play at notrump and denies length in spades, with which a takeout double could have been made.

TAKEOUT CONVENTIONS
The Roth-Stone Double ("Sputnik")

In this convention, also called the Negative Double, a double of an opponent's overcall is for a takeout, not for penalties. It is an essential part of the Roth-Stone system (page 88) and is used in conjunction with some other systems.

1. When an opponent has overcalled partner's opening suit-bid of one, a double is for a takeout, up to and including the four-level.

2. The doubler shows some high-card points but less than enough for a free bid. He should have, in *high-card* points:

At the one-level	**7 to 10 pts.**	With 1 to 2
At the two-level	**7 to 12 pts.**	quick tricks
At the three- or four-level	**9 or more** pts.	With 1 or more quick tricks

SOUTH	WEST	NORTH	EAST	SOUTH	WEST	NORTH	EAST
1 ♣	1 ♡	Double		1 ◇	2 ♡	Double	
		(*takeout*)				(*takeout*)	

North has: ♠ A-8-4-2   *North has:* ♠ J-10-6-2
       ♡ 7-5   ♡ 6-5
       ◇ K-Q-10-4   ◇ 10-6-5-2
       ♣ 8-3-2   ♣ A-K-8

SOUTH	WEST	NORTH	EAST	SOUTH	WEST	NORTH	EAST
Pass	Pass	1 ◇	3 ♡	1 ♠	4 ♣	Double	
Double (*takeout*)						(*takeout*)	

South has: ♠ A-K-10-6   *North has:* ♠ 7-2
       ♡ Q-2   ♡ A-J-10-5
       ◇ Q-J-6-2   ◇ K-9-6-2
       ♣ 10-6-3   ♣ A-5-2

3. The doubler usually has support for both of the unbid suits and asks the opener to rebid in one of those suits if he can; but the doubler may have support for the opener's suit plus one other suit, and occasionally (at a low level) the doubler may have a long, strong suit of his own.

4. The opener may pass for penalties if his secondary strength is in the doubled suit (depending on vulnerability, the bidding level, the opener's defensive strength, etc.) but usually the opener should take out the double. He should select his rebid as follows (in order of preference):

     Bid a new biddable suit
     Rebid a rebiddable suit
     Bid notrump with the opponent's suit stopped

None of these rebids is forcing. With a strong opening bid (17 or more pts.) opener should make a jump rebid; with 19 or more pts. opener may cue-bid as a rebid (bid the opponent's suit).

POINT-COUNT VALUATION

BIDDABLE SUITS

OPENING ONE-BIDS

CHOICE OF SUITS

FORCING BIDS

RESPONSES TO SUIT-BIDS

OPENER'S REBIDS

RESPONDER'S REBIDS

NOTRUMP BIDDING

OPENING 3, 4, 5 BIDS

FORCING TWO-BIDS

OVERCALLS

TAKEOUT DOUBLE

PENALTY DOUBLES

PART-SCORE

DUPLICATE

SLAM BIDS

4-5 NOTRUMP SLAM BIDS

BIDDING CONVENTIONS

PERCENTAGE TABLES

BIDDING SYSTEMS

OPENING LEADS

SIGNALS IN PLAY

COVERING HONORS

FINESSES

SAFETY PLAYS

END-PLAYS SQUEEZE

BRIDGE LAWS

GLOSSARY

TAKEOUT CONVENTIONS (Cont'd)
The Roth-Stone Double (Cont'd)
EXCEPTIONS. A double of an overcall is for penalties, not the "sputnik," when the opening bid was any notrump or preëmptive bid:

SOUTH	WEST	NORTH	EAST	SOUTH	WEST	NORTH	EAST
1 N T	2 ♡	Double		3 ◇	3 ♡	Double	
		(penalty)				*(penalty)*	

However, it is often used as sputnik when 1 N T is overcalled with 2 ♣ or 2 ◇.

Landy Convention
This convention, introduced by Alvin Landy, uses a two-club overcall as a light takeout double of an opponent's notrump bid; therefore a double remains primarily for penalties (page 53). The convention may be used in these situations:

SOUTH	WEST	NORTH	EAST	SOUTH	WEST	NORTH	EAST
1 N T	2 ♣			1 N T	Pass	Pass	2 ♣

SOUTH	WEST	NORTH	EAST
1 ◇	Pass	1 N T	Pass
Pass	2 ♣		

Requirements for Landy two-club bid:

13 to 15 high-card points and 4-4-4-1 distribution, or balanced distribution, and at least one major suit; or

A two-suited hand without good defense against 1 N T

16 or more high-card points and no good lead

With 16 points and a good lead, prefer to double.

Over an opponent's one-notrump bid:

1.	♠ A-10-6-4	♡ K-J-7-3	◇ K-Q-8-2	♣ 9	Two clubs
2.	♠ Q-10-9-2	♡ A-Q-5	◇ Q-9-8-4	♣ A-8	Two clubs
3.	♠ 10	♡ 10-8-7-5-3	◇ A-K-J-10-6-3	♣ 7	Two clubs
4.	♠ K-J-9-4	♡ K-J-5-4	◇ A-9	♣ A-3-2	Two clubs
5.	♠ K-5-2	♡ Q-J-10-9-7-4	◇ A-2	♣ A-3	Double

Astro Convention
This variation of Landy takes its name from Paul *A*llinger, Roger *St*ern and Lawrence *R*osler. The requirements are as in Landy, but the overcalls are:

2 ♣ shows at least 4 hearts, fewer than 4 spades, and at least a 4-card minor suit.

2 ◇ shows 4 or more spades and one other suit of at least 4 cards.

2 N T shows a 2-suiter in the minors.

Over an opponent's one-notrump bid:

On hands 1, 2 and 4 above, bid 2 ◇. On hand 3, bid 2 ♣. On hand 5, double. With

♠ A-7-5   ♡ —   ◇ K-10-9-6-4   ♣ A-K-J-8-3   Bid 2 N T

Continued on next page

TAKEOUT CONVENTIONS (Cont'd)
Ripstra Convention

This is a variation of Landy, proposed by J. G. Ripstra. The takeout is made in the better minor suit, diamonds or clubs, and shows strength in that suit and in both majors. On hands 1 and 2 (p. 73) the takeout bid would be 2 ◇ ; on hand 4 it would be 2 ♣. Partner may pass or bid a major. If partner bids the other minor he must have a very long or strong suit that requires no trump support.

Fishbein Convention

In this convention, created by Harry J. Fishbein, any double of an opponent's opening preëmptive bid (3 or 4 in a suit) is strictly for penalties. A 3 N T overcall of a three-bid is genuine and should be passed. To invite a takeout, the next-higher suit is bid: 3 ◇ over opponent's 3 ♣; 3 ♡ over 3 ◇ ; 3 ♠ over 3 ♡; 4 ♣ over 3 ♠; 4 ◇ over 4 ♣; 4 ♡ over 4 ◇ ; 4 ♠ over 4 ♡; but 4 N T over 4 ♠.

Partner bids his best suit, as in responding to a takeout double (page 53). *Partner may pass* if the Fishbein bid is his best suit and is enough for game, *but he must bid one level higher* if game has not been reached.

Originally the Fishbein takeout bid could be used only by the preëmptive bidder's left-hand opponent, but it has been extended to the reopening hand.

1. SOUTH WEST NORTH EAST   2. SOUTH WEST NORTH EAST
   3 ♣   3 ♡ (*Fishbein*)   3 ◇   Pass Pass 3 ♡
West may have: *East may have:*
1. ♠ K-Q-7-3   2. ♠ K-Q-4
   ♡ A-J-10-5   ♡ A-K-8-6-5-3
   ◇ 5   ◇ 4
   ♣ K-Q-8-5   ♣ K-9-8

CHEAPEST MINOR. This is a variation of Fishbein in which a double is for penalties, an overcall in a major suit or in notrump is genuine, but an overcall in the cheapest minor, as 4 ♣ over 3 ♡ or 3 ◇ over 3 ♣, is for takeout. In the SMITH CONVENTION (of Curtis Smith) only a club bid is used for takeout (as 4 ♣ over 3 ♠) and only by the player at the left of the preëmptive bidder. The reopening bidder uses a double for takeout. Over 4 ♠ or 4 ♡, the takeout bid is 4 N T.

THREE NOTRUMP FOR TAKEOUT. Over an opponent's three-bid a double is for penalties, any overcall in a suit is genuine, but three notrump asks partner to bid. This convention, once widely used, has lost popularity because it prevents a three-notrump contract.

TAKEOUT CONVENTIONS (Cont'd)
Michaels Cue-bids
This convention, devised by Michael Michaels, permits a weak cue-bid with the effect of a takeout double over an opponent's opening minor-suit bid. The cue-bid must be made by the opener's left-hand opponent. He must have:

6 to 11 high-card points
At least 8 cards in the major suits

Partner responds as he would to a takeout double.

1. SOUTH WEST NORTH EAST   *West may have:*
   1 ♣   2 ♣   1. ♠ K-J-7-3   2. ♠ J-9-8-6-4
                       ♡ Q-10-8-4   ♡ A-8-7-3
2. SOUTH WEST NORTH EAST   ◇ Q-9-2   ◇ 6
   1 ◇   2 ◇   ♣ J-5   ♣ Q-J-2

The Michaels cue-bid is used also over an opponent's major-suit opening to show a genuine two-suiter (10 or more cards in two suits), one suit being the other major. There may be more than 11 high-card points, without limit. In responding, partner bids the other major with 3-card or longer support; lacking this, he responds 2 N T to let the cue-bidder show his minor suit.

SOUTH WEST NORTH EAST   *West may have:* ♠ 6-3
   1 ♠   2 ♠   Pass or   ♡ A-K-8-4-2
              Double   ◇ J
                           ♣ K-10-9-6-3

ASTRO CUE-BID. 2 ♣ over 1 ♣ shows a diamond-heart two-suiter; **2 ♠** over 1 ♠ or **2 ◇** over 1 ◇ shows hearts and clubs; **2 ♡** over 1 ♡ shows spades and clubs. Almost always a 6-card minor suit and a 4- or 5-card major.

The SOS Redouble
A player doubled at a one-bid that he cannot stand may show balanced distribution and ask partner to rescue in his best suit by redoubling. This redouble is generally used when a one-notrump bid is doubled but is used also for suit-bids.

1. SOUTH WEST NORTH EAST | 2. SOUTH WEST NORTH EAST
   1 N T Double Pass   Pass | 1 ♣   Double Pass   Pass
   Redouble (SOS) | Redouble (SOS)

In each case the redouble is for takeout. South may hold:
Case 1. ♠ A-K-6   ♡ A-K-5-3   ◇ 10-8-5-4   ♣ J-6
Case 2. ♠ A-10-6-3   ♡ K-Q-6   ◇ 10-7-6   ♣ A-4-2

The redouble bears the SOS message only after a penalty pass. Directly over a double it shows strength.

SOUTH WEST NORTH   EAST | SOUTH WEST NORTH EAST
   1 ♠   Pass   1 N T   Pass | 1 ♠   Pass Pass   Double
   Pass   Double Redouble (*strong*) | Redouble (*strong*)

In each case a bid, rather than a redouble, would show weakness.

POINT-COUNT VALUATION
BIDDABLE SUITS
OPENING ONE-BIDS
CHOICE OF SUITS
FORCING BIDS
RESPONSES TO SUIT-BIDS
OPENER'S REBIDS
RESPONDER'S REBIDS
NOTRUMP BIDDING
OPENING 3, 4, 5 BIDS
FORCING TWO-BIDS
OVERCALLS
TAKEOUT DOUBLE
PENALTY DOUBLES
PART-SCORE
DUPLICATE
SLAM BIDS
4-5 NOTRUMP SLAM BIDS
BIDDING CONVENTIONS
PERCENTAGE TABLES
BIDDING SYSTEMS
OPENING LEADS
SIGNALS IN PLAY
COVERING HONORS
FINESSES
SAFETY PLAYS
END-PLAYS SQUEEZE
BRIDGE LAWS
GLOSSARY

BIDDING CONVENTIONS

On this and the following pages are brief descriptions of certain bidding conventions known in American bridge. Some are of European origin and are more often used in countries other than the United States and Canada. None is used by a great many American players, but all may be encountered here and there in rubber and duplicate bridge.

The Short Club

Nearly all players occasionally bid one club (or one diamond) on an unbiddable suit—a 4-card suit such as 10-x-x-x or a 3-card or even 2-card suit such as K-x-x or A-x. See pages 7 and 9 for examples. *The responder should make no allowances for the possibility that the opening bid was made on a short suit.* The opener will hold a genuine biddable suit in clubs as often as in any other suit. A minor suit is seldom raised to game on less than 5-card support, unless it has been rebid, and raises at lower levels on normal adequate trump support are reasonably safe, even if the opener has a short suit.

Some do play that an opening club bid should be assumed to show a short suit unless it is rebid. No raise may be given without at least a 4-card strong trump holding such as K-Q-x-x. The opener's hand must be quite weak or very strong:

1. ♠ K-Q-J-7   ♡ A-K-Q   ◇ 9-7-4   ♣ A-K-7   Bid one club
Opener bids one club because he cannot bid 2 N T with the diamond suit unstopped and he is afraid a one-spade bid may be passed out.

2. ♠ K-Q-J-7   ♡ J-6-3   ◇ 9-7-4   ♣ A-K-7   Bid one club
Opener bids one club because he might not have a safe rebid if he bid one spade, and he is too weak for 1 N T.

In defense against the short club, some play that an overcall of two clubs is not a cue-bid but shows a genuine club suit.

SOUTH	WEST	NORTH	EAST	*East has:* ♠ 7-5-3
1 ♣	2 ♣	(Genuine)		♡ 8
				◇ K-Q-6
				♣ A-Q-10-9-6-3

Canapé

This method, of French origin, requires the opener to start with the shorter of two suits, sometimes even bidding a strong 3-card suit before a 5- or 6-card suit. The responder can then safely pass the opener's second-bid suit without showing preference. In France, systems incorporating canapé are called "short suit first."

♠ A-K-Q-7-6   ♡ Q-4   ◇ A-10-7-3   ♣ 5-4   Bid one diamond
♠ 9-4   ♡ A-J-7   ◇ 7-3   ♣ A-K-J-10-6-3   Bid one heart

BIDDING CONVENTIONS (Cont'd)
Herbert Convention
This convention, introduced by Walter Herbert, uses the next-higher suit as a negative response to any forcing bid. In the U.S. the convention is chiefly popular in responding to a forcing two-bid.

SOUTH	WEST	NORTH	EAST	
2 ◇	Pass	2 ♡		The 2 ♡ response is used instead of 2 N T to show a weak hand. North does not promise length or strength in hearts.

A 2 N T response may be used to show a genuine suit in the next-higher suit.

Partner makes a forcing 2 ◇ bid. Respond:

♠ 8-6-4-3	♡ 6-2	◇ 7-5-3	♣ 10-8-6-2	Two hearts
♠ 8-6	♡ A-Q-8-7-5	◇ 7-5-3	♣ Q-7-2	Two notrump

The Herbert convention is also used in responding to a takeout double. The lowest possible suit response shows a very weak hand with no preference among the unbid suits and asks the doubler to bid the suit he prefers (or to pass, if he wishes).

SOUTH	WEST	NORTH	EAST	
Pass	1 ♡	Double	Pass	South need not have spades.
1 ♠				He shows weakness and invites North to choose the suit.

Jacoby Transfer Bids
Oswald Jacoby has made popular other transfer bids, at the two-level. If the response to 1 N T is

2 ◇ Responder guarantees a 5-card or longer heart suit; opener must rebid 2 ♡.

2 ♡ Responder guarantees a 5-card or longer spade suit; opener must rebid 2 ♠.

2 ♠ Responder has a minor-suit two-suiter with 14 pts. or more. This is a slam try. Opener rebids in his best minor.

Opener makes a jump rebid of 3 ♡ over 2 ◇, or 3 ♠ over 2 ♡, with a maximum notrump hand and 4 cards in the suit. *Responder may pass opener's rebid* or may rebid. If responder's rebid is:

Game in a suit—opener must pass.

Single raise to 3 ♡ or 3 ♠—opener bids four with support for responder's suit; lacking support, opener passes with a minimum and bids 3 N T with a maximum.

2 N T—with only 2-card support, opener passes with a minimum, bids 3 N T with a maximum; with 3- or 4-card support, opener bids three of the major with a minimum, jumps to four with a maximum.

3 N T—with 2-card support, opener passes; with better support, he bids four in the major.

After a transfer bid, 4 N T by responder is Blackwood.

BIDDING CONVENTIONS (Cont'd)
Asking Cue-bids
These bids are played chiefly on the U. S. Pacific Coast.

A low-level cue-bid (in the opponents' suit, or in a suit in which the bidder cannot have genuine biddable strength) does not show control of that suit but invites partner to bid three notrump if he has at least a partial stopper.

1. South	West	North	East	2. South	West	North	East
1 ◇	Pass	1 N T	Pass	1 ◇	1 ♠	2 ◇	Pass
2 ♣	Pass	2 ♠	Pass	2 ♡	Pass	2 ♠	Pass

In each case South is asked to bid notrump if he has any strength in spades. In the first example, North cannot have a spade suit or he would have responded one spade; in the second, North cannot be strong in spades or he would have bid notrump; in either case, North cannot have a very strong hand or he would not have made, as his first response, a bid that could be passed.

Psychic Controls
Most players use psychic bids infrequently, if ever. Those who do use psychic bids may use one of various devices to identify the psychic when the partner of the psychic bidder has a big hand. There are three conventions in use for this purpose, to be used over partner's jump in a new suit.

1. A rebid in notrump at the lowest level. Any other bid shows a sound opening.

2. A rebid of the original suit or notrump, whichever is the cheaper.

3. The cheapest rebid possible.

South	West	North	East	Having opened a psychic
1 ♡	Pass	3 ♣		heart bid, South would:

1. Rebid 3 N T   2. Rebid 3 ♡   3. Rebid 3 ◇

Fourth Suit Forcing
This convention, which has considerable following among European tournament players but is not accepted by the leading players there, makes a new-suit bid forcing when the other suits have been bid.

South	West	North	East		South	West	North	East
1 ◇	Pass	1 ♠	Pass		1 ◇	1 ♡	1 ♠	Pass
2 ♣	Pass	2 ♡ *Forcing*			1 N T	Pass	2 ♣ *Forcing*	

Bar Bids
According to this convention a rebid in the same suit, after a single raise by partner, is preëmptive and requires partner to pass.

South	West	North	East		South	West	North	East
1 ♡	Pass	2 ♡	Pass		1 ♡	Pass	1 ♠	Pass
3 ♡	Pass	*Must pass*			2 ♣	Pass	3 ♣	Pass
					Must pass			

PERCENTAGE TABLES
Table 1

The chances that the opponents' cards in a suit will be divided in a given way:

YOUR COMBINED HOLDING IN SUIT	OPPONENTS HOLD	OPPONENT'S CARDS WILL BREAK	
11 cards	2 cards	1-1	52 %
		2-0	48 %
10 cards	3 cards	2-1	78 %
		3-0	22 %
9 cards	4 cards	3-1	49.7 %
		2-2	40.7 %
		4-0	9.6 %
8 cards	5 cards	3-2	68 %
		4-1	28 %
		5-0	4 %
7 cards	6 cards	4-2	48.4 %
		3-3	35.5 %
		5-1	14.5 %
		6-0	1.5 %
6 cards	7 cards	4-3	62 %
		5-2	30.5 %
		6-1	6.8 %
		7-0	0.5 %
5 cards	8 cards	5-3	47 %
		4-4	32.8 %
		6-2	17 %
		7-1	2.9 %
		8-0	0.2 %
4 cards	9 cards	5-4	59 %
		6-3	31.4 %
		7-2	8.6 %
		8-1	1 %
		9-0	0.04%

Table 2

The chance that an opponent's honor will be guarded:

ONE OUTSTANDING HONOR WILL BE

YOUR COMBINED HOLDING	UN-GUARDED	GUARDED ONCE ONLY	GUARDED ONLY TWICE	GUARDED THREE TIMES OR MORE
11 cards	52.0%	48%		
10 cards	26.0%	52%	22%	
9 cards	12.0%	41%	37%	10%
8 cards	5.0%	27%	41%	27%
7 cards	2.0%	16%	36%	46%
6 cards	1.0%	9%	27%	64%
5 cards	0.4%	4%	18%	78%
4 cards	0.1%	2%	10%	87%

79

POINT-COUNT VALUATION

BIDDABLE SUITS

OPENING ONE-BIDS

CHOICE OF SUITS

FORCING BIDS

RESPONSES TO SUIT-BIDS

OPENER'S REBIDS

RESPONDER'S REBIDS

NOTRUMP BIDDING

OPENING 3, 4, 5 BIDS

FORCING TWO-BIDS

OVERCALLS

TAKEOUT DOUBLE

PENALTY DOUBLES

PART-SCORE

DUPLICATE

SLAM BIDS

4-5 NOTRUMP SLAM BIDS

BIDDING CONVENTIONS

PERCENTAGE TABLES

BIDDING SYSTEMS

OPENING LEADS

SIGNALS IN PLAY

COVERING HONORS

FINESSES

SAFETY PLAYS

END-PLAYS SQUEEZE

BRIDGE LAWS

GLOSSARY

PERCENTAGE TABLES
Table 3

Distributions of the cards of a suit among the hands of the four players (or of the four suits in one player's hand):

DISTRIBUTION (of Hand or Suit)	%	APPROXIMATE ODDS AGAINST
4–4–3–2	21.6	4 to 1
5–3–3–2	15.5	6 to 1
5–4–3–1	13.	7 to 1
5–4–2–2	10.6	9 to 1
4–3–3–3	10.5	9 to 1
6–3–2–2	5.6	17 to 1
6–4–2–1	4.7	20 to 1
6–3–3–1	3.5	27 to 1
5–5–2–1	3.2	30 to 1
4–4–4–1	3.	33 to 1
7–3–2–1	1.9	50 to 1
6–4–3–0	1.3	75 to 1
5–4–4–0	1.2	80 to 1
5–5–3–0	.9	100 to 1
6–5–1–1	.7	140 to 1
6–5–2–0	.65	150 to 1
7–2–2–2	.5	199 to 1
7–4–1–1	.4	249 to 1
7–4–2–0	.35	275 to 1
7–3–3–0	.25	399 to 1
8–2–2–1	.2	499 to 1
8–3–1–1	.12	850 to 1
7–5–1–0	.11	900 to 1
8–3–2–0	.11	900 to 1
6–6–1–0	.07	1,400 to 1
8–4–1–0	.04	2,499 to 1
9–2–1–1	.02	4,999 to 1
9–3–1–0	.01	9,999 to 1
9–2–2–0	.008	12,500 to 1
7–6–0–0	.006	16,666 to 1
8–5–0–0	.003	33,332 to 1
10–2–1–0	.001	99,999 to 1
9–4–0–0	.001	99,999 to 1
10–1–1–1	.0003	333,332 to 1
10–3–0–0	.0002	499,999 to 1
11–1–1–0	.00002	4,999,999 to 1
11–2–0–0	.00001	9,999,999 to 1
12–1–0–0	.0000003	333,333,332 to 1
13–0–0–0	.0000000006	158,755,357,992 to 1

ITALIAN BIDDING SYSTEMS
The Roman Club

This is one of the systems that have won the world championship an unprecedented number of times for Italy. In this outline the requirements in points refer to high-card points only.

OPENING BIDS. 1 ♣ (artificial and forcing) shows:

> **12 to 16 pts.** and a balanced hand, 4-4-3-2 or 4-3-3-3; or
>
> **21 to 26 pts.** and a balanced hand; or
>
> **A standard forcing two-bid,** especially on a two-suiter such as

♠ A-K-10-8-5-3   ♡ A-Q-9-7-5   ◇ A   ♣ 6   Bid 1 ♣

1 ◇, 1 ♡ or 1 ♠ is bid with a one-suited or two-suited hand including a 5-card or longer suit. With a one-suited hand, bid the long suit—unless the hand has 15 high-card points or more and the suit is too weak to rebid with a jump, in which case bid a 3- or 4-card suit first, a lower-ranking suit if possible but not clubs. With a two-suited hand, open the shorter suit; if the suits are of the same length, bid the lower-ranking unless it is clubs.

♠ K-7-5-3   ♡ 8-4   ◇ A-K-J-9-6-2   ♣ 7   Bid 1 ♠
♠ K-Q-8-7-3   ♡ K-Q-7-5-4   ◇ A-6   ♣ A   Bid 1 ♡

1 N T shows 17 to 20 pts. and 4-4-3-2 or 4-3-3-3 distribution.

2 ♡ or 2 ♠ shows at least 5 cards in the suit bid and at least 4 clubs. With a long diamond suit and 4 clubs, bid 2 N T.

2 ♣ or 2 ◇ shows 4-4-4-1 or 5-4-4-0 distribution: Bid 2 ♣ with 12 to 16 pts., 2 ◇ with 17 pts. or more.

RESPONSES TO 1 ♣. With 0 to 7 pts., respond 1 ◇. A response of 1 ♡, 1 ♠, 2 ♣ or 2 ◇ shows 8 pts. or more, and 2 ♠ or 2 ◇ shows at least a 5-card suit. A response of 1 N T shows a balanced hand with 12 to 15 pts.; 2 N T, at least 16 pts. A 2 ♡ or 2 ♠ response shows 12 pts. or more with a 5-card or longer suit including at least A-K, A-Q, or K-Q.

RESPONSES TO 1 ◇, 1 ♡, OR 1 ♠. Responder may not pass. A single raise or the next-higher bid (as 2 ♡ or 1 ♠ over 1 ♡) are negative responses showing 0 to 8 pts.

RESPONSES TO 2 ♡ OR 2 ♠: Responder may pass with 0 to 6 pts. Any new-suit response is forcing. A preference to 3 ♣ is discouraging. With 6 to

Continued on Next Page

Continued on Next Page

11 pts. and 3-card support, responder should raise; with more points he should bid game. A jump to 4 ♣ invites a game in clubs. If responder bids 2 N T he is asking the opener to clarify his distribution, which opener will do by bidding a 3-card side suit, rebidding a 6-card major, bidding 3 N T to show 5-5-2-1 distribution, or bidding 3 ♣ with 5-4-2-2.

RESPONSES TO 2 ♣ OR 2 ◇. Responder bids his best suit with a weak hand and 2 N T with a strong hand.

RESPONSES TO 1 N T. With a balanced hand and 0 to 5 pts., responder passes. With an unbalanced hand of 0 to 5 pts. responder bids 2 ♣. After the opener's rebid of 2 ◇, the responder passes with diamonds or signs off by bidding two in his own suit.

Responder to 1 N T holds:
♠ 7-5   ♡ J-7-6-5-3-2   ◇ 8-5-4   ♣ 9-5   Bid 2 ♣
Opener rebids 2 ◇, responder bids 2 ♡, opener must pass.

Responder raises to 2 N T with 6 to 8 pts., to 3 N T with 9 or 10 pts., and a balanced hand. Responses of 3 ♡ and 3 ♠ show 6-card suits with 4 or 5 points in the suit and no outside strength. Responses of 2 ♡, 2 ♠, 3 ♣ and 3 ◇ are forcing to game and require the opener to clarify his opening bid and his support for the bid suit. A response of 2 ◇ asks the opener to show a 4-card major. A game bid by the responder ends the auction.

RESPONSES TO 2 N T. Responder may pass with a weak, balanced hand. He may sign off in diamonds by bidding 3 ◇ or in clubs by bidding 4 ♣. A 3 ♣ response asks for opener's distribution and opener will show any 3-card major, bid 3 N T to show 5-5 in minors, bid 3 ◇ with 5-4-2-2, bid 4 ♣ with a 6-card diamond suit.

OPENER'S REBIDS. After opening 1 ♣ with 12 to 16 pts. and receiving a negative response, opener rebids a 4-card major if he has one, or a 3-card heart suit, or 1 N T. If he has opened on 21 to 26 pts., he jumps in notrump. If he has opened 1 ♣ with a standard forcing two-bid, he jumps in a suit. Over a 1 ◇ response he bids only 2 ♣ or 2 ◇ if these are natural bids. Over constructive responses, having the weakest of the 1 ♣ bids, opener jumps in notrump with a maximum and bids a suit with a minimum.

After an opening bid of 1 ◇, 1 ♡, or 1 ♠, the opener may jump in the original suit, or reverse to

ITALIAN BIDDING SYSTEMS (Cont'd)
The Roman Club (Cont'd)

show strength, or may simply rebid his suit to show a minimum. He may rebid in notrump to show a 5-4-2-2 hand with a 5-card minor suit.

If opener bid 2 ♣ or 2 ◇ and received a 2 N T response, he rebids in his *short* suit. If he received a suit response he may pass with a minimum or raise with a maximum. If he does not fit responder's suit, he bids the next-higher-ranking suit and responder will place the contract. For example:

Opener: ♠ A-Q-8-3   ♡ K-10-7-6   ◇ 5   ♣ A-10-4-3
Responder: ♠ K-9-2   ♡ 8-2   ◇ Q-9-6-4-3   ♣ K-7-5

Opener bids 2 ♣, responder 2 ◇; opener bids 2 ♡ to deny diamonds. Responder now bids 2 ♠, his preference among opener's three suits.

OVERCALLS AND DOUBLES. Overcalls are natural. A takeout double shows 12 to 16 pts. and a forced response at one or two shows responder's poorest unbid suit. Responsive doubles are used. A 1 N T overcall is a strong takeout double. An overcall in the opponent's suit is not for takeout but shows ability to play at that suit.

SLAM BIDDING: After a trump suit has been established, new-suit bids are asking bids. Responses are by steps, showing first- or second-round controls in the asked suit. A 4 N T bid is Blackwood with Roman responses (see page 63).

THE NEAPOLITAN CLUB

This is one of the systems that have won the world championship for Italy an unprecedented number of times. In the following outline only high-card points are considered.

OPENING BID OF 1 ♣. Open 1 ♣ on any hand of 17 pts. or more. Distribution does not count, nor does the bid describe the holding; it merely establishes the minimum number of points and is forcing.

Responses to the 1 ♣ Bid. Responder shows the number of controls he holds, counting an ace as two controls and a king as one, without regard to his distribution. A response of 1 ◇ shows no controls; 1 ♡ shows 1; 1 ♠, 2; 2 ♣, 3; 1 N T, 4; 2 ◇, 5; 2 N T, 6 or more. The only variation is with a single ace and no other high cards, when the response is 1 ♡, showing only one control. With no controls but a good suit of six or more cards, responder jumps in that suit.

Continued on Next Page

When Opponent Overcalls Partner's 1 ♣ Bid, pass with no controls. A double is for penalties. Over 1 ◇ overcall, respond one level higher, ranging from 1 ♡ to 2 ◇, or 2 N T with 6 controls; over 1 ♡ overcall, 1 ♠ shows 1 or 2 controls, 1 N T shows 3 controls, etc., up to 2 ♡; over 1 ♠, a 1 N T bid shows stopper and no more than 2 controls; 2 ♣ shows 1 or 2 controls, 2 ◇ shows 3 controls, 2 N T shows 4 or more. Over a 1 N T overcall, same responses. Over two of a suit, 2 N T shows 3 controls, a cue-bid shows 4 or more. Other bids are natural.

Opener's Rebids. A jump in a suit is forcing to game. If opener does not wish to force to game he bids his suits in order of length and rank. A rebid of 1 N T is a natural bid and responder may pass or may seek a possible fit: 2 ♣ over a rebid of 1 N T asks for majors; 3 ♣ over a rebid of 1 N T asks for any 4-card suit; or responder may show a long suit of his own.

OPENING BID OF 1 ◇, 1 ♡, OR 1 ♠. With only one suit, bid it; with two suits of equal length, bid the higher-ranking first; with two suits of unequal length, bid the shorter first, unless the shorter suit is lower in rank in a minimum hand, or is clubs, in which case bid the long suit first.

Responses to opening suit-bids other than clubs or notrump: Pass with 5 pts. or less. Bid any biddable suit at the one-level rather than 1 N T. With 10 pts., it is possible to bid a new suit at the two-level. With 5 to 10 pts. and 4 cards in partner's suit, raise that suit. With 9 to 12 pts. and a fit, use a jump raise, which is nonforcing. The 1 N T response indicates 5 to 10 pts. and no suit biddable at the one-level.

OPENING BID OF 1 N T. With a biddable hand but fewer than 17 pts., balanced distribution, and no biddable suit other than clubs, bid 1 N T.

♠ 7-6-4	♡ A-K-J	◇ 9-5-2	♣ K-Q-J-7	Bid 1 N T
♠ 7-4	♡ A-K-J	◇ 5-2	♣ K-Q-J-7-5-3	Bid 1 N T

Responses to 1 N T. Responder passes with a balanced hand and 0 to 8 pts. With stoppers in diamonds, hearts, and spades, he responds 2 N T with 10 or 11 pts.; 3 N T with 12 pts. or more. A 2 ◇ response requires the opening notrump bidder to bid 2 ♡. A response of 2 ♡ or 2 ♠ is forcing for one round, while a jump bid in either major is forcing to game and shows a semi-solid suit. A response of 2 ♣ is a weak hand, 5 to 10 pts. with 3 or

ITALIAN BIDDING SYSTEMS (Cont'd)
The Neapolitan Club (Cont'd)

more clubs. With 3 or more clubs and 12 pts. or more, responder forces with a 3 ♣ bid.

OPENING BID OF 2 ♣. This is usually a strong two-suited hand containing 5 clubs or more but not strong enough for a 1 ♣ bid; or a one-suiter not adapted to a 1 N T opening.

♠ K-Q-10-7-5	♡ K-3	◇ —	♣ A-10-8-6-4-3	Bid 2 ♣
♠ A-6	♡ K-8	◇ 7-5	♣ K-Q-10-7-6-5-3	Bid 2 ♣

Responses to 2 ♣ Opening. Responder passes with 0 to 5 pts. A 2 ◇ response is conventional and asks for the second suit in opener's hand; if opener's second suit is diamonds, he bids 2 N T over responder's 2 ◇. With a good suit responder may bid 2 ♡ or 2 ♠, either of which is forcing. With 10 to 11 pts. and a balanced hand the response is 2 N T; with 12 or more pts., 3 N T, holding stoppers in the unbid suits. With 3-card support and 5 to 9 points responder raises to 3 ♣. With a semi-solid suit and a good hand responder jumps in his own suit (forcing to game).

PREËMPTIVE OPENING BIDS. An opening bid of 3 ◇, 3 ♡ or 3 ♠ shows no defensive strength and a long suit without top honors. An opening bid of 3 ♣ shows a strong club suit, and possibly some outside strength—a hand not suitable for a 1 N T bid and not strong enough for a 2 ♣ bid.

♠ 6-4	♡ 5	◇ Q-8-5-3	♣ A-K-Q-J-7-5	Bid 3 ♣
♠ 6-3	♡ 5-4	◇ 8-2	♣ A-K-J-10-8-7-4	Bid 3 ♣

With a semi-solid suit of 7 cards, headed by the A-K or A-Q-J, in diamonds, hearts, or spades, and no side honors, bid 2 N T. Over a 2 N T opening responder must bid 3 ♣ and opener shows his suit.

OVERCALLS AND DOUBLES. Overcalls are normal. The Herbert Convention (page 68) is used in response to a takeout double. Over a 1 N T overcall (16 to 18 pts.) the Stayman Convention is used. A 2 N T overcall shows a 5-5 two-suiter: over 1 ♣ it shows diamonds and hearts; over 1 ◇, clubs and hearts; over 1 ♡ or 1 ♠, diamonds and clubs. A jump 2 N T overcall is preëmptive; partner responds 3 ♣ to let overcaller show his suit.

SLAM BIDDING. A jump bid of 4 N T is Blackwood. An unnecessary jump bid in a suit is an asking bid and the responses are: cheapest response lacking second-round control; one step higher with king or singleton; next step higher with ace or void; next step higher with A-K.

BRITISH BIDDING SYSTEMS
Acol System

This system, used by many famous British players including Terence Reese, resembles Standard American bidding but one-bids are more limited; jump bids are used more often and are less often forcing. The name comes from a bridge club that flourished on Acol Street, London, in the 1930s.

OPENING BIDS of one in a suit are made on

> Any hand containing 14 or more high-card points
>
> Any 13-pt. hand unless you are vulnerable and hold 4-3-3-3, in which case a pass is optional
>
> Any 12-pt. hand with a 5-card suit
>
> Any 10- or 11-pt. hand containing a 6-card suit or two 5-card suits

If partner bids 2 N T over the opening bid, a rebid of the suit is a sign-off.

A double raise in the suit (1 ♡—3 ♡) is not forcing; nor need opener's reverse bid be strong.

OPENING NOTRUMP BIDS. For 1 N T, 12 to 14 pts. not vulnerable; 15 to 18 pts. vulnerable. For 2 N T, 22 to 24 pts. For 3 N T, a long, solid minor suit with one or two stoppers or partial stoppers in the other suits.

Responses to opening N T bids. Two of a suit, discouraging. The Stayman Convention is used over 1 N T or 2 N T to ask for a major. Otherwise: Raise 1 N T if the combined hands may have 26 pts. Raise 2 N T with 4 pts.; any suit takeout is forcing. Any response to a 3 N T bid is a slam try.

TWO-BIDS. The artificial 2 ♣ bid is used on very strong hands, especially with balanced distribution. Intermediate 2 ♢, 2 ♡ and 2 ♠ bids (page 47) are used; they show 8 playing tricks and are forcing for one round.

Responses to Two-bids. To 2 ♣, the negative response is 2 ♢; to an intermediate two-bid, 2 N T is the negative response. Any other response shows at least 1 honor-trick. After a negative response the responder may pass a rebid of the original suit. A jump shift shows a solid suit.

JUMP RESPONSES. A jump takeout in a new suit (2 ♡ over partner's 1 ♢, or 3 ♣ over partner's 1 ♡) is forcing to game but may show only 15 pts. or even less if responder is willing to insist on reaching game. A double raise is *not* forcing (see

POINT-COUNT
VALUATION

BIDDABLE
SUITS

OPENING
ONE-BIDS

CHOICE
OF SUITS

FORCING BIDS

RESPONSES
TO SUIT-BIDS

OPENER'S
REBIDS

RESPONDER'S
REBIDS

NOTRUMP
BIDDING

OPENING
3, 4, 5 BIDS

FORCING
TWO-BIDS

OVERCALLS

TAKEOUT
DOUBLE

PENALTY
DOUBLES

PART-SCORE

DUPLICATE

SLAM BIDS

4-5 NOTRUMP
SLAM BIDS

BIDDING
CONVENTIONS

PERCENTAGE
TABLES

BIDDING
SYSTEMS

OPENING
LEADS

SIGNALS
IN PLAY

COVERING
HONORS

FINESSES

SAFETY PLAYS

END-PLAYS
SQUEEZE

BRIDGE LAWS

GLOSSARY

BRITISH BIDDING SYSTEMS (Cont'd)
Acol System (Cont'd)

page 19) nor is a jump response of 2 N T, which may be made on 11 to 14 pts.

SLAM BIDDING. The Culbertson 4-5 Notrump Convention is used, and the Grand Slam Force.

CAB SYSTEM

This is a system used by many of the leading British players. The name comes from the system's use of the two-*C*lub bid, *A*ce-showing responses, and *B*lackwood.

TWO-BIDS. An opening 2 ♣ bid is artificial and is forcing. Partner responds 2 ◇ with no ace; 2 ♡, 2 ♠, 3 ♣, 3 ◇ holding the ace of that suit; 3 N T with two aces; 2 N T with 8 pts. including two kings. A later bid of 4 N T by the 2 ♣ bidder is Blackwood asking for kings.

Intermediate two-bids (page 47) are used and are forcing for one round. The negative response is 2 N T.

OPENING ONE-BIDS are limited only in denying enough for an intermediate two-bid. A double raise or jump 2 N T response is forcing for one round, except over an intervening bid. A two-level response requires 10 pts. in high cards; opener rebids 2 N T to show a minimum.

OPENING ONE-NOTRUMP BID—16 to 18 pts. Gladiator responses (which originated in New Zealand) are used. With 1 honor-trick responder bids 2 ♣, which requires the opener to rebid 2 ◇; responder then signs off in his best suit. A 2 ◇ response is game-forcing and asks the opener to bid a 4-card major suit. A 2 ♠ or 2 ♡ response is game-forcing and promises at least 5 cards in the bid suit and at least 1½ honor-tricks.

SOUTH	WEST	NORTH	EAST	*North holds:* ♠ 5-4-2
1 N T	Pass	2 ♣	Pass	♡ Q-10-8-6-4
2 ◇	Pass	2 ♡	Pass	◇ K-4
Pass				♣ Q-7-2

The CAB opening 3 N T bid is based on a long minor suit (known to most Americans as the "gambling 3 N T").

♠ A ♡ J-5 ◇ A-K-Q-J-8-7-4 ♣ K-4-2 Bid 3 N T

Opening three-bids require 6 playing tricks, not vulnerable, and 7 playing tricks, vulnerable.

♠ 8 ♡ Q-J-10-9-7-5-2 ◇ A-4 ♠ 7-3-2 Bid 3 ♡, NV
♣ 7-3 ♡ A-Q-J-9-8-4-2 ◇ Q-J-10 ♣ 7 Bid 3 ♡, vul.

87

ROTH-STONE SYSTEM

The Roth-Stone bidding system was introduced about 1946 by Alvin Roth and Tobias Stone. It has had a great effect on expert bidding methods in America. Essential departures from Standard American practice include:

SOUND (STRONG) OPENING BIDS. An opening bid shows at least 14 pts. including at least 11 pts. in high cards and at least 2 defensive tricks. An opening bid in a major suit by an unpassed hand guarantees at least a 5-card suit. A short minor suit may be bid, lacking a 5-card major.

RESPONSES. *To a major suit:* Bid 1 N T (forcing) with 6 to 11 pts. Raise once with at least 3 trumps and 10 to 12 pts. (other responses possible); double raise with at least 4 trumps and 13 or more pts. (A double raise is preferred to a temporizing—two-over-one or one-over-one—bid.) Any response of two in a lower-ranking suit shows at least 11 pts., usually more, and guarantees a rebid after opener's second bid. *To a minor suit:* Responder must show a 4-card major if he has one, unless he can bid 2 ♣ over 1 ◇. A response of 1 N T is not forcing. *All the foregoing assumes that responder did not pass originally.*

JUMP RESPONSES—preëmptive, showing a hand with less than 6 pts. and no more than 2-card trump support.

Partner bids 1 ◇, next hand passes.
♠ 7-6-3   ♡ Q-J-10-9-7-4   ◇ 6-5   ♣ Q-7   Respond 2 ♡

OPENER'S REBID OVER 1 N T RESPONSE. [Having bid a major] opener may rebid a 6-card suit, bid a 4-card side suit, or if necessary bid a 3-card minor suit. A direct raise of responder's one-over-one response guarantees 4 trumps.

WEAK TWO-BIDS. Only a 2 ♣ bid is forcing. Every other two-bid (2 ◇, 2 ♡, 2 ♠) is weak, showing 6 to 12 high-card pts. (because of the American Contract Bridge League's rule). Requirements vary with vulnerability conditions:

1st or 2nd Hand, not vulnerable *vs.* vulnerable:
♠ 6-3   ♡ 7-6   ◇ Q-J-9-8-7-3   ♣ K-8-5   Bid 2 ◇

1st or 2nd Hand, vulnerable *vs.* not vulnerable:
♠ K-Q-J-9-8-4   ♡ 6-3   ◇ A-7-5   ♣ 8-2   Bid 2 ♠

3rd Hand, not vulnerable, or equal vulnerability:
♠ 7-4   ♡ K-J-8-6-5-3   ◇ 8-5-4   ♣ Q-5   Bid 2 ♡

RESPONSES TO WEAK TWO-BIDS. The only forcing response is 2 N T. A response in a new suit may show strength but is prepared for a pass by

POINT-COUNT
VALUATION

BIDDABLE
SUITS

OPENING
ONE-BIDS

CHOICE
OF SUITS

FORCING BIDS

RESPONSES
TO SUIT-BIDS

OPENER'S
REBIDS

RESPONDER'S
REBIDS

NOTRUMP
BIDDING

OPENING
3, 4, 5 BIDS

FORCING
TWO-BIDS

OVERCALLS

TAKEOUT
DOUBLE

PENALTY
DOUBLES

PART-SCORE

DUPLICATE

SLAM BIDS

4-5 NOTRUMP
SLAM BIDS

BIDDING
CONVENTIONS

PERCENTAGE
TABLES

BIDDING
SYSTEMS

OPENING
LEADS

SIGNALS
IN PLAY

COVERING
HONORS

FINESSES

SAFETY PLAYS

END-PLAYS
SQUEEZE

BRIDGE LAWS

GLOSSARY

ROTH-STONE SYSTEM (Cont'd)

opener. A raise in the bid suit or a jump in a new suit (as 3 ♠ over partner's opening 2 ♠ or 2 ♡) is preëmptive and must be passed by opener.

OPENING 2 ♣ BID. The artificial, game-forcing 2 ♣ bid is used, with 2 ◇ the negative response. A 2 N T rebid by opener shows 25 or 26 pts.; a 3 N T rebid, more than 26 pts.

OPENING NOTRUMP BIDS. An opening bid of 1 N T shows 16 to 18 pts. in high cards and 4-3-3-3 or 4-4-3-2 distribution but is never bid with two 4-card majors. An opening bid of 2 N T shows 22 to 24 pts. An opening bid of 3 N T is based on a long, solid minor suit such as A-K-Q-x-x-x and stoppers or partial stoppers in at least two, preferably all three of the other suits—but it is a preëmptive bid; for example

♠ K-5   ♡ 7   ◇ A-K-Q-9-7-6-2   ♣ Q-4-3   Open 3 N T

RESPONSES TO NOTRUMP BIDS. Extended Stayman is used, with 2 ♣ and 2 ◇ responses. Transfer bids are used, at four-level only.

Over 2 ♣ response to 1 N T, opener shows any 4-card major; lacking one, bids 2 ◇. Over 2 ◇ response (forcing to game), opener shows any 4-card major, bids 2 N T with two 4-card minors, and if unable to make one of these responses bids his 4-card minor.

A 4 ◇ response calls for 4 ♡, a 4 ♡ response for 4 ♠. A response of 4 ♠ is genuine and should be passed. A 4 ♣ response is Gerber. Any other jump response (3 ♣, 3 ◇, 3 ♡, 3 ♠) is weak and preëmptive (in uncontested bidding). Any nonjump bid in competition is weak.

OVERCALLS. Jump overcalls, as 2 ♡ over opponent's 1 ◇ or 3 ♣ over opponent's 1 ♠, are weak. Any simple overcall, as 2 ♠ over 2 ♡, is strong. A cue-bid overcall (as 2 ♣ over left-hand opponent's 1 ♣; 2 ♠ over 1 ♠, etc.) serves as a light, distributional takeout double. Both 2 ♣ and 2 ◇ are takeout bids over opponent's N T bid, in any position, and also over a 1 N T response (not over a 1 N T rebid); 2 ♣ guarantees spades, 2 ◇ hearts.

ROTH-STONE DOUBLE (page 72) is used up to the four-level. It is often used to differentiate between a strong and weak single raise.

RESPONSIVE DOUBLES (page 54) are used over either a raise or a suit-bid. A double is for a takeout through the three-level; at the four-level it is optional.

KAPLAN-SHEINWOLD SYSTEM

This bidding system, by Edgar Kaplan and Alfred Sheinwold, follows Standard American practice except in the following special cases.

WEAK NOTRUMP. The opening bid of 1 N T, vulnerable or not vulnerable, shows 11 to 14 pts., with balanced distribution.

♠ 8-3 ♡ K-7-6-4 ◇ A-Q-8-2 ♣ K-J-6 Bid 1 N T

Partner may jump to game with 12 or more points and balanced distribution, or may bid game in a suit with 10 pts. or more in high cards and a suit playable opposite a weak doubleton. In general, responder will pass balanced hands up to 11 pts.; but may raise to 2 N T with 11 pts. and a 5-card minor suit headed by a high card.

Responder uses the Stayman Convention (non-forcing) and Gerber (direct jump to 4 ♣).

A jump response of 3 ♣ or 3 ◇ is preëmptive, typically showing a 6-card suit and fewer than 10 pts. in high cards. A jump to 3 ♠ or 3 ♡ is forcing to game.

5-CARD MAJORS. An opening bid of 1 ♠ or 1 ♡ promises a 5-card or longer suit. A response of 1 N T is forcing for one round. Opener rebids a 6-card major or a 4-card or longer side suit; with no side suit he bids his lowest-ranking 3-card suit.

Holding ♠ A-K-J-6-5 ♡ 7-2 ◇ K-8-5 ♣ Q-6-3
Bid 1 ♠ and, if partner responds 1 N T, rebid 2 ♣.

Partner raises a major suit with three trumps and about 6 to 9 pts., including distributional support. With 3 trumps and 10 or 11 pts., he responds 1 N T first and jumps in the major at his next turn. With 4 trumps and 10 or 11 pts., responder jumps immediately to three of the major (invitational, but not forcing). With 4 trumps and 12 to 15 pts., responder jumps to 3 N T (which opener *must* take back to four of the major if he has no slam ambitions).

ANY SUIT RESPONSE IS FORCING. A response in a new suit at the level of two is usually taken to game. When responder has a good suit but no side strength, he may bid and rebid his suit to indicate his lack of game-going strength. When responder's suit is long but topless and his hand is mediocre (below 10 pts. in high cards), he may first respond 1 N T and later bid his suit.

OPENING MINOR-SUIT BIDS. The opening bid of 1 ♣ or 1 ◇ is never shaded. If balanced, the hand must be of 15 pts. or more (too strong for a weak notrump); if unbalanced, the hand must be

KAPLAN-SHEINWOLD SYSTEM (Cont'd)

a sound opening bid (12 pts. or better) with a natural rebid. An opening bid of 1 ♣ or 1 ◇ must often be made on a 3-card suit.

♠ A-J-8-3   ♡ K-Q-7-6   ◇ A-J-5   ♣ 9-2   Bid 1 ◇
The hand is too strong for 1 N T, and a major-suit bid would promise a 5-card suit.

An opening bid of 1 ♣ or 1 ◇ followed by a rebid of 1 N T shows 15 to 17 pts. in high cards. Responder may treat the rebid as a strong opening 1 N T and use the Stayman Convention in responding. An opening in a minor suit followed by a raise of responder's major suit promises four trumps and 15 to 17 pts. (including distributional points).

INVERTED MINOR RAISES. Responder's double raise in a minor is weak, typically showing at least 5 trumps, no 4-card or longer major suit, and a maximum of 8 pts. in high cards.

Responder's single raise in a minor is forcing for one round, promising trump support with at least 9 pts. in high cards, and denying a 4-card major.

TWO-BIDS. Weak two-bids in spades, hearts, and diamonds. In first or second position, the weak two-bid promises a strong 6-card suit in a hand that is not quite worth an opening bid of one. In third or fourth position, the suit may be weaker.

A raise to three of a weak two-bid made in first or second position is preëmptive. A response in a new suit or 2 N T is natural and forcing for one round. A raise of a 3rd- or 4th-hand two-bid is strong; any other response is natural, not forcing.

An opening bid of 2 ♣ shows a game-going hand in a suit, or at least enough for two notrump. Negative response is 2 ◇; any other response is strength-showing. Opener's rebid of 2 N T shows 23 or 24 pts.; a jump to 3 N T shows 25 or 26 pts.

Opening bid of 2 N T shows 21 or 22 pts. Opening bid of 3 N T shows similar point count but includes a minor suit that will deliver 5 fast tricks.

PREËMPTIVE BIDS. Opening bids of three virtually guarantee no defensive strength. Any jump overcall shows a topless suit without side strength.

♠ K-J-10-7-6-3   ♡ 5-2   ◇ 6   ♣ 8-7-4-3
Bid 2 ♠ over opponent's opening bid of 1 ♣, 1 ◇, or 1 ♡.

A jump-shift response to partner's opening bid is preëmptive if an opponent has bid or doubled or if the opening bid was made third- or fourth-hand.

CONVENTIONS USED: Negative doubles, responsive doubles, unusual notrump, psychic opening bid on 2 to 5 pts. and length in the bid suit.

VANDERBILT CLUB SYSTEM

Harold S. Vanderbilt, who created the modern game of Contract Bridge in 1925, also introduced the first bidding system, based on an artificial opening bid of one club to show a strong hand and an artificial one-diamond response to deny high-card strength in the responder's hand. The system is called the "Vanderbilt Club" or "Club Convention."

The One-Club Bid

One Club is the opening bid with a strong suit-type hand (unbalanced distribution, or strength concentrated in a long, strong suit), if the hand contains either 16 or more high-card points and 5 or more offensive tricks (winners), or 1 or 2 fewer high-card points and 2 or 3 more offensive tricks.

♠ A-K-Q-10-7-5-3	♡ A-8	◇ K-5	♣ 7-6	Bid 1 ♣
♠ 6	♡ A-K-J-6-2	◇ K-J-8-3	♣ A-Q-4	Bid 1 ♣
♠ 7-4-2	♡ A-10	◇ A-K-Q-J-5-3	♣ 8-2	Bid 1 ♣

One diamond is the negative response, showing any hand of any type on which a positive response cannot be given.

Partner opens one club. Respond:

♠ 6-4-2	♡ 7-5-3	◇ 6-5-4	♣ 8-6-4-2	One diamond
♠ K-Q-10-8-7-5-3-2	♡ 6-3	◇ 5-4	♣ 6	One diamond

Positive Responses. Any response to one club except one diamond guarantees a holding of at least: 2 aces; or 3 kings; or A, K, and Q; or 2 kings + 2 queens; or a 6-card or longer suit headed by A-K or better. A positive response (any response except one diamond, except in competitive bidding), is *forcing to game*. In addition to guaranteeing the high-card values specified in this paragraph, the following positive responses show:

1 ♡, 1 ♠, 2 ♣ or 2 ◇: A natural, but strong, one-over-one response.

2 ♡, 2 ♠, 3 ♣ or 3 ◇: A solid 5-card or longer suit.

3 ♡, 3 ♠, 4 ♣ or 4 ◇: A 6-card or longer suit requiring only A, K or Q to make it solid (for example, K-Q-J-10-x-x, A-Q-J-10-x-x or A-K-J-10-x-x) plus sufficient outside strength to qualify for a positive response.

1 N T: A good hand wth notrump-type distribution.

2 N T: A hand with at least one top honor (A, K or Q) in every suit, and slam possibilities opposite a strong one-club bid.

VANDERBILT SYSTEM (Cont'd)

Effect of an Overcall or Double of a 1 ♣ Bid.
If the opening one-club is overcalled or doubled, the responder's action is as follows:

1. A double of an overcall, or a redouble of a double, is a positive response. A jump bid in no-trump means the same as over a pass except that it guarantees a stopper in the suit of the overcall.

South bids 1 ♣. West bids 1 ♡. North's action:
♠ A-Q-6-3   ♡ 7-2   ◇ A-5-3   ♣ 9-6-3-2   Double
♠ A-6   ♡ K-7   ◇ A-8-6-5-3-2   ♣ K-6-5   2 N T

2. A minimum notrump response is encouraging but not forcing and shows a stopper in the suit of the opponent's overcall.

South bids 1 ♣. West bids 1 ♡. North holds:
♠ 6-5   ♡ K-9-3   ◇ K-7-5-4   ♣ Q-6-4-3   1 N T

3. A minimum suit response is encouraging but not forcing and shows a genuine suit.

South bids 1 ♣. West bids 1 ♡. North holds:
♠ A-Q-6-5-3   ♡ 7-4   ◇ J-8-4   ♣ 7-6-3   One spade

4. A jump suit response is forcing for one round only.

South bids 1 ♣. West bids 1 ♡. North holds:
♠ K-Q-10-8-6-3   ♡ 7-4   ◇ Q-10-5   ♣ 6-3   Two spades

Other Opening Bids

Limited Opening Bids. Opening bids of 1 ◇, 1 ♡, 1 ♠ and 2 ♣ have the same minimum requirements in high-card points as do opening suit-bids of one in other systems (page 6), *but the high-card point range is limited to about 6 pts.*—about half as much range as in other systems—because with a strong hand 1 ♣ is bid.

For the opening 2 ♣ bid at least a 5-card suit containing 5 pts. is required. If no other bid is available, open 1 ◇ on a 3-card suit containing at least 5 pts.

♠ A-Q-6-5-2   ♡ K-6   ◇ A-5-3   ♣ 8-6-4   One spade
♠ 8-6-4   ♡ K-6   ◇ A-5-3   ♣ A-Q-6-5-2   Two clubs
♠ 8-6-4   ♡ A-6   ◇ A-K-7   ♣ K-7-5-3-2   One diamond

Opening Bids with Notrump-Type Hands. Open:

1 N T with **16** to **18** pts. (the usual standard requirement).

1 ♣ with **19** or **20** pts.; rebid 1 N T over a 1 ◇ response.

2 N T with **21** or **22** pts.

1 ♣ with **23** or **24** pts.; rebid 2 N T over a 1 ◇ response.

1 ♣ with 9 probable winners including a stopper in every suit; rebid 3 N T over a 1 ◇ response.

Continued on next page

VANDERBILT SYSTEM (Cont'd)

3 N T with 8 or 9 probable winners, most of them in minor suits. This bid is partly preëmptive and is best made third hand after two passes.

♠ 8-5 ♡ K-6 ◇ A-K-Q-10 ♣ A-K-Q-J-10 Bid 3 N T, third hand

Opening Suit-Bids of Two and Three. 1. An opening bid of 2 ♠, 2 ♡, and (except for expert use*) 2 ◇ is the weak two-bid (page 46).

2. An opening bid of 3 ♣ or 3 ◇ shows a solid 7-card suit (exceptionally, a 6-card solid suit) and invites partner to bid 3 N T with the other suits stopped.

3. Opening 3 ♠ and 3 ♡ bids are preëmptive, showing 7 winners; the suit need not be solid.

♠ K-4	♡ 6-2	◇ A-K-Q-J-8-5	♣ 7-5-3	Bid three clubs
♠ A-4	♡ 6-2	◇ A-K-Q-J-8-5	♣ 7-5-3	Bid one club
♠ Q-J-10-7-5-3	♡ 6-2	◇ A-8	♣ 7-5-3	Bid two spades
♠ Q-J-10-8-7-5-3	♡ 6-2	◇ A-8	♣ 7-5	Bid three spades

Two notrump is the only forcing response to a weak two-bid. Responses to major-suit three-bids are game tries, as in Standard American. In response to a minor-suit three-bid, three notrump invites a pass and any other response suggests a game.

Stayman Convention—used over opening no-trump bids and over notrump rebids by the player who opened 1 ♣ and received a 1 ◇ response. If the partnership auction (the opponents always passing) goes: Opener 1 ♣, responder 1 ◇; opener 1 N T (19 or 20 pts.), responder 2 ♣ (Stayman); opener must show a 4-card major if possible. But if responder bids 2 ♠ or 2 ♡, instead of 2 ♣, opener must pass, because of responder's failure to use Stayman before bidding 2 ♠ or 2 ♡.

Blackwood or Gerber. Use whichever is cheaper. Since a 1 ♣ opening does not show a bona fide club suit, it does not prevent the subsequent use of a Gerber 4 ♣ bid to ask for aces.

---

*For expert use, Mr. Vanderbilt recommends an opening, forcing-to-game 2 ◇ bid on very strong hands (usually a hand with a void or singleton and a solid or nearly solid suit) calling for specific aces on the first round and, if opener desires, specific kings on the second round and specific queens on the third round.

♠ A-K-J-9-7-5-2 ♡ A-Q-6 ◇ — ♣ A-K-5 Bid 2 ◇
If responder holds: ♠ Q-6 ♡ K-8-4 ◇ 8-6-5-2 ♣ Q-7-6-2 the partnership auction would go: 2 ◇ (specific aces?), 2 ♡ (no ace); 2 ♠ (specific kings?—because the cheapest suit), 3 ♡ (king of hearts); 3 ♠ (specific queens?—because the cheapest suit), 5 ♣ (two queens of same color—they must be black since opener holds ♡ Q); 7 ♠ by opener.

POINT-COUNT
VALUATION

BIDDABLE
SUITS

OPENING
ONE-BIDS

CHOICE
OF SUITS

FORCING BIDS

RESPONSES
TO SUIT-BIDS

OPENER'S
REBIDS

RESPONDER'S
REBIDS

NOTRUMP
BIDDING

OPENING
3, 4, 5 BIDS

FORCING
TWO-BIDS

OVERCALLS

TAKEOUT
DOUBLE

PENALTY
DOUBLES

PART-SCORE

DUPLICATE

SLAM BIDS

4-5 NOTRUMP
SLAM BIDS

BIDDING
CONVENTIONS

PERCENTAGE
TABLES

BIDDING
SYSTEMS

OPENING
LEADS

SIGNALS
IN PLAY

COVERING
HONORS

FINESSES

SAFETY PLAYS

END-PLAYS
SQUEEZE

BRIDGE LAWS

GLOSSARY

SCHENKEN CLUB SYSTEM

The Schenken System was devised by Howard Schenken, by most experts considered the all-time greatest player. The Schenken System is based on the Vanderbilt Club Convention (page 92) and on various methods originated by Mr. Schenken. In the Schenken System standard preëmptive and defensive tactics, opening no-trump bids and responses (including the Stayman Convention), and one-bids (limited), are used; areas of dissimilarity are as follows. Only high-card points are specified.

Opening One-Club Bid—strong and artificial. One-club opening bids are made on:

A. Balanced strong hands of 17 to 23 points.

♠ 6-3 ♡ A-J-10-4 ◇ A-Q-8-3 ♣ A-Q-6 Bid 1 ♣
Unsuitable for 1 N T because of the weakness in spades.

♠ A-J-7 ♡ A-Q-5 ◇ K-J-7-6 ♣ A-8-2 Bid 1 ♣
Too strong for 1 N T, too weak for 2 N T.

B. Unbalanced strong hands, 14 points minimum.

Bid 1 ♣ on:

♠ A-K-Q-J-6-3	♡ 5	◇ K-J-7	♣ A-7-3	18 pts.
♠ K-Q-J-7-5-4	♡ 5	◇ A-3	♣ A-K-8-4	17 pts.
♠ 4	♡ A-K-Q-8-5-3	◇ A-Q-10-5	♣ 7-6	15 pts.
♠ A-K-10-9-5	♡ A-Q-J-6-3	◇ 8-4	♣ 5	14 pts.

This hand is opened 1 ♣ only because both suits are majors.

With ♠ 4 ♡ A-Q-10-8-3 ◇ A-Q-10-7-6 ♣ K-8 Bid 1 ◇

Responses to One Club. A. Bid one diamond, the negative response, artificial but forcing, with less than 9 points.

B. With 9 points or more including 1½ quick tricks, respond naturally:

1 N T—balanced hand, 9 to 11 points
2 N T—balanced hand, 12 or 13 points
3 N T—balanced hand, 14 or 15 points
1 ♠ or 1 ♡—5-card or strong 4-card suit
2 ◇ or 2 ♣—usually 5-card or longer suit

Single jump response—solid suit; for example, A-K-Q-J-x, A-K-Q-10-x-x, A-K-Q-x-x-x-x.

Double jump response—nearly solid suit; for example, K-Q-J-x-x-x or A-Q-J-10-x-x (with at least one side trick).

Rebids by One-Club Bidder. A. After a forced 1 ◇ response: **1.** One of a major or two of a minor is not forcing. **2.** A (single) jump rebid is forcing for one round. **3.** One notrump shows 19 or 20 points, or a strong 18 points such as

♠ K-Q-J-10 ♡ A-10-7 ◇ A-6-3 ♣ A-10-5

4. Two notrump shows 21 or 22 points.

Continued on next page

SCHENKEN SYSTEM (Cont'd)

B. After a natural positive response: **1.** Over a 1 N T or 2 N T response, 2 ♣ or 3 ♣ respectively is Stayman (page 36). **2.** Over one of a suit, except 1 ◇, a single jump rebid shows a solid suit and a double jump rebid shows a nearly solid suit, as described above.

Rebids by Responder. 2 ♣ over 1 N T or 3 ♣ over 2 N T is Stayman; any other rebid is natural, but if the first response was positive any rebid short of game is forcing and game must be reached.

When Opponents Bid Over 1 ♣. 1. If an opponent overcalls at the one- or two-level, a double by responder is for takeout but shows enough strength for a positive response. **2.** If an opponent doubles, a redouble shows enough for a positive response. **3.** A cue-bid in the opponent's suit shows enough for a positive response. **4.** A suit-bid shows less than 9 points and is not forcing.

Opening Bid of 1 ♠, 1 ♡ or 1 ◇. These show limited hands, usually 12 to 16 points, sometimes as low as 10 or 11 points.

♠ A-K-7-5-4	♡ A-7-3	◇ 8-4-2	♣ J-5	Bid 1 ♠
♠ 6	♡ A-J-10-4	◇ K-Q-8-2	♣ Q-10-5-4	Bid 1 ♡
♠ K-7-5-3-2	♡ A-7-3	◇ A-8-4	♣ J-5	Pass (suit too weak)
♠ K-Q-J-10-7-6	♡ 6-2	◇ A-J-5	♣ 8-6	Bid 1 ♠
♠ K-Q-J-7-6	♡ K-Q-10-8-6	◇ 6-5	♣ 4	Bid 1 ♠
♠ K-7-4	♡ A-6-3	◇ Q-J-6	♣ K-10-7-6	Bid 1 ◇

(Three-card diamond suits are often bid.)

Hands with 14 points in high cards *must* be opened. Hands with 16 points are maximum.

Responses to 1 ♠, 1 ♡ or 1 ◇. All responses are constructive. Responder should pass with 8 points or less. **1.** A notrump takeout shows a balanced hand and: 1 N T, 9 to 11 pts.; 2 N T (not forcing) 12 or 13 pts.; 3 N T, 14 or 15 pts. **2.** A one-over-one response shows 8 pts. or more. **3.** Two in a lower-ranking suit shows 10 pts. or more but can be shaded with a good 6-card suit. **4.** A single jump shift (as 3 ♣ over 1 ♠) is a game force and a *mild* slam invitation, usually showing 15 pts. or more with strong distribution.

Opening Bid of 2 ♣. This is a limited bid, showing a 6-card suit or strong 5-card suit with 11 to 15 points.

♠ 8-5	♡ K-J-6	◇ A-6-3	♣ K-Q-J-8-4	Open 2 ♣
♠ A-6-4	♡ 7-6	◇ A-5	♣ Q-J-10-9-7-5	Open 2 ♣
♠ 8-5	♡ K-J-6	◇ A-Q-6	♣ K-J-8-6-4	Open 1 ◇

A suit takeout in response to an opening two-club bid is not forcing. A response of 2 N T, or a single jump takeout, is forcing.

SCHENKEN SYSTEM (Cont'd)

Opening Bid of 3 ♣. This shows a solid suit, with 10 to 15 points in the hand. It is not forcing.

Opening Bid of 2 ♦. This is a strong artificial opening bid, forcing to game. It shows: A. A balanced hand with 23 points or more. B. A freak hand with a long suit and slam possibilities.

♠ K-Q-J-10-7-6-3   ♡ 4   ◇ 7   ♣ A-K-Q-5   Open 2 ◇

Responses to 2 ◇. Ace-showing responses are used. 1. With no ace, respond 2 ♡. 2. With the ♡ A, respond 2 N T. 3. With one of the other aces, bid the suit. 4. With two aces, jump in the higher-ranking suit. 5. With three aces, double-jump in the highest-ranking suit.

Rebids by 2 ◇ Bidder. Cheapest rebid asks for kings unless responder has shown two or three aces, in which case cheapest rebid in diamonds asks responder to show his second-highest ace.

Weak Jump Overcalls are used.

Weak Two-bids in Majors (opening 2 ♠ or 2 ♡) show: 6-card suit headed by Q-J or better, usually 8 to 12 points; or 5-card suit headed by K-Q-10 or better, 8 to 12 points.

Responses to Weak Two-bids. Two notrump is the only forcing response. A suit response may be passed.

Opening Bid of 2 N T. This shows a solid suit in a hand of 17 to 20 points with potential stoppers (usually A, K or Q) in the other suits. A 3 ♣ response is Gerber, asking for ace-showing rebids. Raises are: 3 N T shows 5 to 10 pts.; 4 N T, 11 or 12 pts.; 6 N T, 13 to 15 pts. An opening 3 N T bid is the same but shows 17 to 22 pts. with 8 or 9 probable winners. A response of 4 ♣ is Gerber.

Other Club Systems

VIENNA SYSTEM. A one-club bid shows the weakest opening hand, 11 to 16 points. The negative one-diamond response shows fewer than 8 points; a suit response is made with 8 to 10 points; with 11 or more points the responder must bid one notrump (forcing), regardless of his distribution.

BOLAND CLUB. (For Vincent Boland.) The Vanderbilt Club requirements are used, but if the opening one-club bidder's first rebid is in clubs he shows that he had a natural, possibly minimum club bid, not a strong, artificial bid.

POINT-COUNT VALUATION

BIDDABLE SUITS

OPENING ONE-BIDS

CHOICE OF SUITS

FORCING BIDS

RESPONSES TO SUIT-BIDS

OPENER'S REBIDS

RESPONDER'S REBIDS

NOTRUMP BIDDING

OPENING 3, 4, 5 BIDS

FORCING TWO-BIDS

OVERCALLS

TAKEOUT DOUBLE

PENALTY DOUBLES

PART-SCORE

DUPLICATE

SLAM BIDS

4-5 NOTRUMP SLAM BIDS

BIDDING CONVENTIONS

PERCENTAGE TABLES

BIDDING SYSTEMS

OPENING LEADS

SIGNALS IN PLAY

COVERING HONORS

FINESSES

SAFETY PLAYS

END-PLAYS SQUEEZE

BRIDGE LAWS

GLOSSARY

THE CARD TO LEAD

The following table tells only the *card* to lead, after the *suit* to lead has been selected. For guidance in selecting the suit to lead, see pages 100 to 104. The leads shown below are time-honored and, though there are some modern variations, should be used in the absence of an understanding with partner.

CONVENTIONAL LEADS

HOLDING IN SUIT	LEAD AT SUIT BIDS	LEAD AT NOTRUMP
A-K-Q-J *alone or with others.*	K, then J	A* then J
A-K-Q *with 3 or more others.*	K, then Q	A, then K
A-K-Q-x-x *without a reëntry.*	K, then Q	Fourth best
A-K-Q-x-x *or* A-K-Q-x.	K, then Q	K, then Q
A-K-J-x-x-x-x *or more*	K, then A	A, then K
A-K-10-x-x-x-x *or more*	K, then A	A, then K
A-K-J-10-x-x *with a reëntry*	K	A
A-K-J-10 *alone or with others.*	K	K
A-Q-J-x-x-x-x *or* A-Q-J-10-x-x *with a reëntry*	A	A
A-K-J, A-K-10, A-K *in 4-, 5-, or 6-card suit*	K, then A	Fourth best
A-Q-J-x *or longer*	A	Q
A-Q-10-9 *or longer*	A	10
A-J-10-x *or longer*	A	J
A-10-9-x *or longer*	A	10
A-x-x-x *or longer*	A	Fourth best
A-K-x	K, then A	K, then A
A-K *alone*	A, then K	Avoid
K-Q-J *alone or with others*	K, then J	K, then Q
K-Q-10 *alone or with others.*	K	K
K-Q-x-x-x-x-x *(7 cards) or more*	K	K
K-Q-x-x-(x-x)	K	Fourth best
K-Q-x	K	K
K-Q *alone*	K	Avoid
K-J-10-x *or longer*	J	J

*Traditionally, the lead of an ace in an unbid suit against a notrump contract is conventional, requesting that partner follow suit with his highest card, even a king or queen, unless dummy reveals that the sacrifice of such a card would eventually lose a trick or a stopper. Many players still follow this traditional rule, but there is a growing tendency to open ace from A-K against notrump contracts, and when this method is used the old rule of following suit with the highest card must be abandoned. Also, the lead of a king against notrump traditionally called for the play of partner's second-highest card, but this rule was always of doubtful value and in any case has been generally abandoned.

THE CARD TO LEAD (Cont'd)

HOLDING IN SUIT	LEAD AT SUIT BIDS	LEAD AT NOTRUMP
K-10-9-x or longer..........	10	10
Q-J-10 alone or with others..	Q	Q
Q-J-9 alone or with others...	Q	Q
Q-J-x-x-x-x (7 cards).....	Q	Q
Q-J-x-x-(x-x).............	Q	Fourth best
Q-J-x....................	Q	Q
Q-J alone.................	Q	Q
Q-10-9-x or longer.........	10	10
J-10-9 alone or with others..	J	J
J-10-8 alone or with others..	J	J
J-10-x...................	J	J
J-10 alone................	J	J
J-10-x-x or more..........	J	Fourth best
10-9-8 alone or with others..	10	10
10-9-7 alone or with others..	10	10
10-9-x-x or more..........	10	Fourth best
10-9 alone or 10-9-x alone...	10	10
Any 4-card or longer suit not listed above.........	Fourth best	Fourth best

LEADS IN PARTNER'S BID SUIT

A-x, K-x, Q-x, J-x, 10-x, or any other Doubleton......	High card	High card
J-10-x, 10-x-x or x-x-x......	Highest *	Highest
A-J-x, A-x-x, K-J-x, K-x-x, Q-10-x, Q-x-x, J-x-x......	Highest *	Lowest
Q-J-x-(x).................	Q	Q
A-x-x-x or better...........	A	Fourth best
K-Q-x-(x).................	K	K
Any other 4 or more cards..	Fourth best	Fourth best

LEADS IN UNBID SHORT SUITS *

x-x	Q-x-x	K-x-x	K-10-9	A-10-9
x-x-x	Q-10-x	K-J-x	A-x-x	A-J-x
J-x-x	Q-10-9	K-10-x	A-10-x	A-J-10

*Many expert players have adopted the policy of always leading the lowest card from any 3-card suit, such as 7-5-3 or even 4-3-2, whether or not the suit was bid by partner. This is a controversial issue and the majority of the experts probably still lead the highest card, or the middle card from a holding such as 8-7-3 (so that on the second trick the highest card can be played to show that the lead was not from a doubleton). In practice there is little if any advantage to either method of leading. However, from a 3-card holding headed by *two* honors (counting the ten as an honor) it is better to lead one of the honors against a notrump contract if the object is to establish a long suit in partner's hand. The lead of the low card will often block the suit. If dummy seems likely (from the bidding) to have a singleton, king should be led from K-J-x and queen from Q-10-x. If dummy's singleton is the next-lower honor, the card led will cover it; if dummy's singleton is the next-higher honor, the suit would have been blocked anyway.

OPENING LEADS AT NOTRUMP

To defeat a notrump contract, it is almost always necessary to establish a long suit. The following four general principles govern notrump leads.

1. In general try to open the longest and strongest suit in the combined hands.

Unless partner has bid, your own longest suit should usually be opened.

But if your longest suit has been bid by an opponent, do not open it unless it is long and solid (such as Q-J-10-9-x, K-Q-J-8-x, etc.).

2. If partner has bid a suit usually open that suit *unless*

(a) You have a singleton in partner's suit and a good suit of your own to lead; or

(b) You have a long solid suit and enough reëntries to defeat the opponents' contract alone (for example, K-Q-J-x-x with an Ace or King outside).

Likewise, if *you* have bid a suit and *partner has raised it*, it is probably your best opening lead.

3. If partner *doubles* the opponents' notrump bid, observe these rules:

If *partner* has bid a suit, open partner's suit.

If *you* have bid a suit and partner has *not*, open *your* suit.

If neither you nor partner has bid a suit, open a suit which *dummy* has bid *but not rebid*, and which declarer *has not raised*.

Otherwise, open as though partner had not doubled.

It is a popular convention in leading when partner has doubled a 3 N T contract that the lead must be in the first suit bid by dummy. This convention applies when neither defender has bid.

SOUTH	WEST	NORTH	EAST
1 ♣	Pass	1 ♠	Pass
2 ♣	Pass	2 ◊	Pass
2 N T	Pass	3 N T	Double

According to the convention cited, West must open a spade. Other players permit West to open any suit but clubs.

4. With a very weak hand, open a worthless 3-card suit or even a worthless doubleton.

You would probably never get in to run a long suit even if you could establish it.

Sometimes, even with a strong 4-3-3-3 or 4-4-3-2 hand, and no leadable sequence, a worthless short suit is a good *waiting lead*, so that declarer will have to lead to you in your strong suits.

BEST NOTRUMP LEADS
In Order of Preference

In the following table the suit-holdings are preferred in the order in which they are numbered; the conventional card to lead from each particular suit-holding is underlined. See also the tables on pages 98-99.

The <u>CARD</u> to lead is underlined

1. An established suit (*lead the Ace*).
2. <u>A</u>-K-J-x-x-x-x *or better.*
3. <u>A</u>-K-Q-10-x, A-<u>K</u>-Q-x, A-<u>K</u>-Q-x-x. *But from A-K-Q-x-x lead fourth best with no entry* if partner probably has one.*
4. A-<u>Q</u>-J-10-x-x, A-<u>Q</u>-J-x-x-x-x. *But with a sure entry,* lead Ace.*
5. <u>K</u>-Q-J-x-(x-x)
6. A-<u>K</u>-x-x-x-x-x, <u>K</u>-Q-x-x-x-x-x, or <u>Q</u>-J-x-x-x-x-x (*7-card suit*).†
7. Q-<u>J</u>-10-x-x (*or more*).
8. A-K-x-<u>x</u>-x-x, A-Q-x-<u>x</u>-x-x, A-J-x-<u>x</u>-x-x, K-Q-x-<u>x</u>-x-x (*5-card or 6-card suits*).
9. Q-J-10-<u>x</u>, <u>K</u>-Q-10-x, Q-J-9-x-x *or more.*
10. Any six-card suit *with an entry.**
11. Q-x-x-<u>x</u>-x, J-10-x-<u>x</u>-x *or better, with an entry.**
12. <u>J</u>-10-9-x, Q-10-x-<u>x</u>, x-x-x-<u>x</u>-x, *or better, with an entry.**
13. x-x-x-<u>x</u> (*from strong hands only*).
14. <u>x</u>-x-x, <u>10</u>-x-x, <u>J</u>-10-x.
15. <u>x</u>-x, <u>J</u>-10, <u>10</u>-x (*not Q-x or higher*).
16. <u>Q</u>-J-x, <u>K</u>-Q-x, A-<u>K</u>-x (*usually avoid*).

AVOID THE FOLLOWING LEADS
In the ordered named
(Except as gambling *desperation leads*).

1. Doubleton honor leads.
2. Three-card suits headed by one high honor, or two honors not in sequence.
3. Four-card suits headed by only the Ace, King or Queen, without Jack or 10.
4. Weak five-card suits in entryless hands.

---

*An Ace, a King, and often a Q-J-x is a reasonably certain entry.
†Many players now lead ace from A-K suit against notrump; see page 86.

POINT-COUNT VALUATION

BIDDABLE SUITS

OPENING ONE-BIDS

CHOICE OF SUITS

FORCING BIDS

RESPONSES TO SUIT-BIDS

OPENER'S REBIDS

RESPONDER'S REBIDS

NOTRUMP BIDDING

OPENING 3, 4, 5 BIDS

FORCING TWO-BIDS

OVERCALLS

TAKEOUT DOUBLE

PENALTY DOUBLES

PART-SCORE

DUPLICATE

SLAM BIDS

4-5 NOTRUMP SLAM BIDS

BIDDING CONVENTIONS

PERCENTAGE TABLES

BIDDING SYSTEMS

OPENING LEADS

SIGNALS IN PLAY

COVERING HONORS

FINESSES

SAFETY PLAYS

END-PLAYS SQUEEZE

BRIDGE LAWS

GLOSSARY

HOW TO CHOOSE YOUR LEAD
Against Trump Contracts

The opening lead, being "blind," often loses a trick. *The most desirable lead is usually one that is safe.*

Best leads: An A-K-Q, or a long suit headed by A-K (*lead the King*). You will win the first trick and can see dummy to guide your choice of a second lead, yet you still retain one or more *stoppers* in the suit. With A-K-x or even A-K-x-x, the lead is not so good, as it may sacrifice a valuable stopper (*see example on page 51*). Any solid sequence (K-Q-J, Q-J-10, etc.) or a suit bid by partner (in which he probably has the high cards) is also a preferred lead.

Worst leads: A lead from a suit headed by honors *not in sequence* (such as A-Q) usually sacrifices a trick. *Avoid such suits* except when the bidding indicates that declarer's side has two long, solid suits which will give him his contract when run. *In such cases you must cash all winning cards immediately.*

Waiting leads: The lead of a worthless suit *cannot directly lose a trick.* The only damage it can do is to lose *time*—that is, waste a lead in which the defenders might establish or cash winning cards. Lacking a safe honor lead, usually lead a worthless short suit—including a 2- or 3-card holding in trumps.

Avoid, in most cases, any suit bid by the opponents, even though in that suit you have A-K or K-Q-J.

THE SLAM-LEAD CONVENTION

The slam-lead or slam-double convention was first proposed by Theodore A. Lightner and often is called the Lightner Slam Double.

Any double of a slam contract—trump or notrump—warns the doubler's partner *not* to make his normal lead, such as the suit he or his partner has bid.

Your partner may double a trump slam when he is void in some suit and can ruff the opening lead. Holding a particularly long suit, even though it has been bid by the opponents, consider this possibility.

Or, your partner may have A-Q in a suit dummy has bid. Ordinarily, you would expect dummy to have the principal strength in this suit. If partner doubles a slam, consider opening such a suit.

No rigid rule, such as leading the first suit bid by dummy, does or should govern the choice of the opening leader. His hand is a better guide than any rule.

BEST OPENING LEADS
Against Trump Contracts
IN ORDER OF PREFERENCE

In the following table the suit-holdings are preferred in the order in which they are numbered; the conventional card to lead from each particular suit-holding is underlined. See also the tables on pages 98-99.

(Numbers refer to notes on next page.)

1. A-K-Q, A-K-J, A-K-x-x-x *with or without others.*

2. A trump *when Declarer has bid strongly in two suits, of which Dummy has supported only one.*

3. A or A-K *alone, with sure entry to Partner's hand and at least one small trump.*

4. K-Q-J (-x-x-x)

5. A-x, K *or singleton[1] of Partner's suit.*

6. Singleton *with trump entry and at least one ruffer.*

7. Q-J-10 *or more, with no probable entry.*

8. Partner's suit, *with 4 or less. (See page 62).*

9. Q-J-10 *or more, with or without an entry.*

10. J-10-9-x *with or without others.*

11. A-K-x-x or A-K-x[2]

12. K-Q-10 *with or without others.*

13. Singleton *with 3 or more ruffers.*

14. Doubleton *containing no honor.*

15. A-x *with trump entry or when Partner has bid strongly.*

16. A or A-K *alone.*

17. 10-9-8-x

18. J-10-8-x

19. Trump x-x-x, x-x, A-x-x, K-x-x—*not a singleton.*

20. *Any suit which your partner has supported.[3]*

21. J-10, J-10-x, or Q-J *alone.*

22. A-x-x—*underlead A-x-x, A-x-x-x when bidding indicates that Dummy has a strong hand with balanced distribution.*

23. 10-9-7-x

24. x-x-x *

*Many players now lead the lowest card from any 3-card holding; see the note to page 88.

Continued on next page

25. x-x-x-x̱	32. J-x-x-x̱-(x)
26. Q-J-9-x̱	33. Q-J-x (x-x)
27. Ḵ-Q-x-x-x	34. A̱-x-x-x-x or more
28. J-10-x-x	35. K-x-x̱
29. Ḵ-x-x-x̱-(x)	36. Q-10-x̱
30. Q-x-x-x̱-(x)	37. 10̱-x-x
31. 10-x-x-x̱-(x)	

[1]A singleton or opponents' suit should not be led except when the object is to get a ruff.

[2]A-K-x is often not so good as other leads ranked below it in this classification.

[3]A suit headed by A-Q or A-J should usually not be opened, unless partner has supported it very strongly.

[4]The ten is the traditional lead; the lowest card is the modern lead from 10-x-x, and many players lead the lowest from any three cards, however low: See the footnote to page 99.

LEADS TO BE AVOIDED

A-Q or A-Q-J	K-J-x or K-J-10-x
Singleton trump	A-J-x or A-J-10
Q-x-x or J-x-x	K-Q-x or K-Q-x-x
Q-x or J-x	K-x
A-x except as in case 15	K alone

A suit bid by the opponents

Any one of these leads may be correct when the bidding situation so indicates.

LEADS AGAINST SLAM BIDS

Either six- or seven-bids. Exceptions are marked (*).
See also "The Slam-Lead Convention."

	SUIT SLAM	NOTRUMP
Singleton.............	Good*	Very bad
Sequence of 3 honors...	Good	Good
Partner's suit.........	Good	Good
Ace.................	Fair**	Very bad**
Doubleton...........	Fair	Fair
Sequence of 2 honors...	Fair*	Bad
Trump 10-x-x or x-x-x..	Good	
Trump J-x, 10-x, x-x or x	Bad	
Q-x-x-x-x-x or lower....	Good	Fair
K-x-x-x or Q-x-x-x.....	Fair*	Very bad
x-x-x or x-x-x-x........	Fair	Fair

*Very bad against Grand Slams. **Very good against Grand Slams.

DEFENDERS' SIGNALS

In discarding, a player should be careful not to sacrifice a necessary guard to an honor. (An Ace requires no guard, but if unguarded may cause the suit to be blocked.) Discards and follow-suit plays can also signal valuable information to partner, as follows:

Encouraging Signals. Play (or discard) an *unnecessarily high card, not your lowest.* This (called the *come-on*) tells partner to lead, or continue leading, the suit. When possible, next play (or discard) a *lower* card—this is a *high-low*, or *echo*, and confirms your previous encouraging card. With a doubleton, if you want to ruff a third round, play high-low.

Discouraging Signals. The play (or discard) of your *lowest* card in a suit warns partner *not* to lead it. Do not, however, sacrifice a possible trick-winner or stopper solely to make an encouraging play or a high-low signal. Sometimes, low discards in *other* suits may steer partner to a suit in which you cannot conveniently give a come-on signal.

Distributional Echoes. To play high-low *in the trump suit* tells partner *you still have a trump left*, and (usually) that you want to ruff a lead in some other suit. Do not high-low in trumps without at least three trumps.

In a suit partner has led against a notrump contract, when you cannot attempt to win the first trick, play high-low from three or more cards (5 from 7-5-4) and the lower from a doubleton (3 from 8-3).

When following suit to the opponents' strong suit, having only worthless cards or cards you can spare, first play your *lowest* card if you have *three cards* or *five cards* in the suit; play high-low if you have *two cards* or *four cards* in the suit. In starting the high-low signal from a 4-card holding, either of the middle cards may be played (from J-7-5-2, either the seven or the five but not the deuce).

The Suit-Preference Signal.* When leading a card for partner to ruff; or when following suit or discarding, *provided the card played cannot logically be one of the signals described above;*

The play of a *very high* card tells partner next to lead the *higher-ranking available suit* (other than trumps);

The play of a *low* card calls for the *lower-ranking* of those suits.

* Developed by Hy Lavinthal of Trenton, New Jersey

DEFENDERS' PLAYS

Conventional Follow-Suit Plays

On partner's low-card lead, usually play your highest card or *the lowest equivalent of your highest card.*

With Q-10-6, dummy holding J-3-2, if dummy plays low, play the 10, not the Queen. With Q-10-9, play the 9, not the 10. With K-Q-x, play the *Queen*, etc.

Remember. you *lead* the *highest* of equals, but you *play* the *lowest* of equals.

"Finesses Against Dummy"

When dummy has an honor, and you have a *higher* honor, in the suit led, usually *save your higher honor* to cover dummy's honor when it is played. In this table, assume dummy's lowest card to be played:

DUMMY HOLDS	YOU HOLD	PARTNER LED	PLAY
K-x-x-(x)	A-J-x A-10-x A-9-x A-J-10	x	J 10 9 10
Q-x-x-(x)	A-J-x A-J-10 K-10-x K-9-x	x	J 10 10 9
J-x-x	Q-9-x K-10-x K-9-x	x	9 10 9
A-J-x	K-10-x Q-9-x	x	10 9

The Rule of Eleven

When you can assume your partner's lead to be his fourth-best, you may apply the Rule of Eleven:

Subtract the denomination (number of pips) of the card led from 11.

The result is the number of cards higher than the card led, held by other three players.

Then, since you know how many higher cards you hold, and can see the dummy, you can easily determine the declarer's holding.

When you can count (or infer) more higher cards in the other three hands than there could be under the Rule of Eleven, the lead is probably a short-suit lead.

The Uppercut

In trumping a trick that declarer may overtrump, usually trump high. Your high trump will force out a higher trump from declarer, perhaps establishing a trump card in partner's hand.

106

WHEN TO COVER AN HONOR

Usually, when declarer leads an honor from his own hand or dummy, and you have a higher honor in the same suit, you should cover with your honor if you believe partner may hold a combination such as J-x, 10-x-x-x, 9-x-x-x, Q-9-x, etc.

An honor led from a doubleton in dummy, such as Q-x, should not be covered if you might sacrifice a sure later stopper in the suit, as with K-x-x-x.

If Jack is led from J-x do not cover with Queen if declarer may have K-10 and partner may have the Ace.

The table gives the play that is *usually* correct.

DUMMY HOLDS	YOU HOLD	CARD LED	PLAY
Q-J-10-(x-x)	K-x-x-(x)	Queen	Low, all leads
Q-J-9-x-x	K-x-x	Queen, then Jack	Low, both leads
Q-J-9-x	K-x-x or K-10-x	Queen, then Jack	Low, first lead, cover second
Q-x-(x-x)	K-x-(x-x)	Queen	cover*
J-10-x-x-x	K-x-x or Q-x-x	Jack, then 10	Low, both leads
J-10-x-x	A-Q-9	Jack	cover
J-10-x	K-x-x or Q-x-x	Jack, then 10	Low, first lead, cover second
J-x-(x-x) or 10-x-(x-x)	K-x-x or Q-x-x	Jack or ten	cover*
10-x-x-(x) or 10-9-x-(x)	J-x-x-(x)	10	low
J-x-x	K-Q-x	Jack	cover
A-x-x-(x)	K-x-x-(x)	Queen or Jack	low
A-x-x-(x)	Q-x-x-(x)	Jack	low
A-x-x-(x)	K-9-x	Queen or Jack	Cover Queen Low on Jack
A-x-x	K-10-x	Queen or Jack	Cover Queen Low on Jack
A-x-x or K-x-x	Q-x-(x) or J-x-(x)	10	low
Q-x-x	J-x-x	10	low

* When partner may have a singleton in the suit, do not cover.

HOW TO FINESSE

To develop as many trick-winning cards as possible from the combined suit holdings of your hand and dummy, the mathematically correct methods are:

STRAIGHT LEADS

It is always best to lead toward a high card (that is, from the hand that does not contain the high card). However, with sequences of three or more honors, such as King, Queen, and Jack, or Queen, Jack, and ten, one or more tricks may be established by leading the honors and letting the opponents take their higher cards.

PLAYS FOR A DROP

With **nine** or more cards in the combined hands, including Ace and King, lead out the Ace and King. (With nine cards, when the opponents have the Queen, the play for a drop is mathematically *slightly* better than a finesse, lacking contrary information from the bidding).

With **eleven** cards in the combined hands, including the Ace, lead the Ace. But with ten cards or less including A-Q, finesse as described below.

HOW TO FINESSE

With the following holdings, usually finesse. Extra low cards in either hand seldom affect the correct play.

YOU AND DUMMY HOLD:		WHAT TO DO
IN ONE HAND	IN OTHER HAND	(If Intervening Opponent Plays Low)
A-Q	x-x	Lead toward A-Q. Play Q.
A-Q-10	x-x-x	Lead toward A-Q-10. Play 10. This may win 3 tricks or assure 2 tricks. If 10 loses to J, play same as A-Q.
A-Q-9	x-x-x	Lead toward A-Q-9 and play 9. This will win extra trick if J-10 are under A-Q-9 and K is required to beat 9. If 9 loses to J or 10, play same as A-Q.
A-K-J	x-x-x	Cash the Ace. Later, lead toward K-J. Play J.
A-K-10	x-x-x	Lead toward A-K-10. Play 10. This will win extra trick if Q-J are under A-K-10.

HOW TO FINESSE (Cont'd)

YOU AND DUMMY HOLD:		WHAT TO DO
A-J-10	**x-x-x**	*Lead toward A-J-10. Play 10. This will probably lose to K or Q. Next lead toward A-J. Play J, finessing for other honor.*
A-J-9	**x-x-x**	*Lead toward A-J-9. Play 9. This is an effort to find 10 and one honor at the right. If 9 is won by Q or K, next lead toward A-J and play J.*
A-x-x	**Q-x-x or Q-J-x-x**	*Cash Ace, then lead toward Q.*
A-x-x (Or A-x and Q-J)	**Q-J-10**	*Lead Q. Play low from A-x.*
A-K-Q-10	**x-x**	*Play Ace, then lead toward K-Q-10 and play 10. (But with seven or more cards of suit play for a drop.)*
K-x	**x-x**	*Lead toward K-x. Play the K.*
K-x-x	**J-10-9**	*Lead J. Play low from K-x-x.*
K-Q-10	**x-x-x**	*Lead toward K-Q-10. Play K. Next lead toward Q-10. If the K won the first trick, play Q. If the K lost the first trick, play 10.*
K-J-x	**x-x-x**	*Lead to K-J-x and play J. If it loses to Q, see play of K-x above. With a doubleton in either hand, play either K or J on first round.*
K-10-x	**Q-x-x**	*Lead toward Q. Play Q. Next lead toward K-10. Play 10.*
K-10-x or **Q-10-x**	**x-x-x**	*Lead toward high cards. Play 10. Next lead toward K-x (or Q-x) and play K (or Q).*
K-x-x	**Q-x-x**	*Lead toward either honor. Play the honor. If it wins, next lead toward other honor but play low.*
Q-J-x	**x-x-x**	*Lead toward Q-J-x. Play J. Next lead toward Q-x. Play Q.*
Q-x-x	**J-9-x**	*Lead toward Q-x-x. Play Q. Next lead toward J-9. Play 9.*

POINT-COUNT VALUATION

BIDDABLE SUITS

OPENING ONE-BIDS

CHOICE OF SUITS

FORCING BIDS

RESPONSES TO SUIT BIDS

OPENER'S REBIDS

RESPONDER'S REBIDS

NOTRUMP BIDDING

OPENING 3, 4, 5 BIDS

FORCING TWO-BIDS

OVERCALLS

TAKEOUT DOUBLE

PENALTY DOUBLES

PART-SCORE

DUPLICATE

SLAM BIDS

4-5 NOTRUMP SLAM BIDS

BIDDING CONVENTIONS

PERCENTAGE TABLES

BIDDING SYSTEMS

OPENING LEADS

SIGNALS IN PLAY

COVERING HONORS

FINESSES

SAFETY PLAYS

END-PLAYS SQUEEZE

BRIDGE LAWS

GLOSSARY

SAFETY PLAYS

A safety play is any method (usually a finesse) used by declarer to limit his loss or to guard against unlikely but damaging distributions. Some so-called safety plays are not wholly safe and better fit the title "percentage plays."

When you can afford to lose *one trick* in the suit, but not *two*, play these holdings as follows:

IN ONE HAND	IN OTHER HAND	WHAT TO DO
A-K-8-x-x (or A-K-8-x & 10-x-x-x)	10-x-x	*Play Ace. If either opponent plays Q, J or 9, next lead low toward 10-x.*
A-Q-10-x-x (9 cards in combined hands, however distributed)	x-x-x-x	*Lead toward A-Q-10. If Jack shows up, play Queen; otherwise play Ace. Next lead toward Q-10.*
A-10-x-x-x (or A-9 and K-10)	K-9-x-x	*Lead low from either hand. Unless opponent shows out, play 9 (or 10) from other hand.*
K-J-x-x (or K-J-x-x-x and A-9-x, etc.)	A-9-x-x	*Take King. Then lead low toward A-9. Play 9 (unless opponent shows out.)*

With the following holdings, the play described is correct in all cases.

IN ONE HAND	IN OTHER HAND	WHAT TO DO
A-Q-x-x	x-x-x-x	*Play Ace. Then lead toward Q-x-x.*
A-9-x-x	Q-10-x-x	*Lead low toward A-9. Finesse 9. If it loses to Jack, next lead Queen and finesse.*
A-10-x-x-x (or the equivalent)	K-x-x	*Play King. Then lead toward A-10 and finesse 10.*
A-K-9-x-x (or the equivalent)	Q-x-x-x	*First, play Queen. Proper play will then be apparent.*
A-Q-9-x-x	J-x-x-x-x	*Lead Jack. Finesse (unless covered).*
A-Q-8-x-x	J-x-x-x	*Lead low toward A-Q. Finesse Q.*
A-K-9-x-x (or the equivalent)	Q-10-x-x	*Take Ace (or King). Further proper play will then be apparent.*

Lacking entries, play as instructed on pages 108-109.

ENTRY PLAYS
Entry-Making Plays

1. **Overtaking** partner's winning card in order to gain the lead.

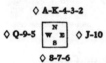

◇ 10-8-6-3

◇ K   ◇ A-Q-J

◇ 9-7-5-4-2

West leads the ◇ King, which would win the trick; but East overtakes with the ◇ Ace in order to be in the lead to cash the Queen and Jack. This saves an entry for East, who would otherwise be forced to gain the lead by winning a trick in another suit.

2. **Unblocking** by playing or discarding an unnecessarily high card, in order to establish a card in partner's hand as an immediate or eventual winner. If in Example 3 above, North had played the five, six and seven of diamonds on the first three leads, South could have won the fourth trick with the ◇ 3, thus retaining the lead.

3. **Ducking** (playing a losing card) on a trick you are able to win, in order to make use of your winning cards in the suit at a later time, when they will be valuable as entries.

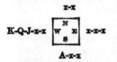

◇ A-K-4-3-2

◇ Q-9-5   ◇ J-10

◇ 8-7-6

South leads the ◇ 8; North ducks by playing the ◇ 2. Now when North later takes the ◇ A-K, the suit will be established and North will remain in the lead to cash the established cards.

Entry-Killing Plays

The Hold-up. First in importance is the hold-up play. A hold-up play is a refusal to win the first (or following) leads of a suit, in order to exhaust one opponent's cards of that suit.

x-x

K-Q-J-x-x   x-x-x

A-x-x

When West leads this suit, South purposely loses the first two leads and wins the third with his Ace. By so doing, he has killed the value of an entry in East's hand—only an entry in West's hand can allow the established cards of the suit to be cashed.

Avoidance Plays. If you have a choice of establishing one of two suits, play the suit in which, if a trick must be lost, it will more probably be lost to the opponent who cannot make a destructive lead.

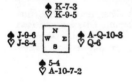

♠ K-7-3
♡ K-9-5

♠ J-9-6   ♠ A-Q-10-8
♡ J-8-4   ♡ Q-6

♠ 5-4
♡ A-10-7-2

There are no trumps. South leads the ♡ 2; West plays low; North ducks with the ♡ 9 in order to put the lead in East's hand. East cannot lead spades without establishing North's King; but if West could lead East and West could win four spade tricks.

END-PLAYS

An end-play is so called because it usually occurs in the last few tricks. Most bridge problems are based on end-plays. There are three main types of end-play: the throw-in, the trump pick-up or "coup," and the squeeze.

The Throw-in

This is usually called simply an end-play, sometimes an *elimination play* or a *strip-and-endplay*. It consists of forcing an opponent to lead at a time when any lead he can make will cost his side a trick. Examples:

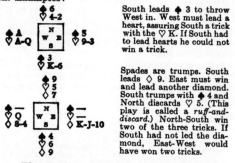

South leads ♠ 3 to throw West in. West must lead a heart, assuring South a trick with the ♡ K. If South had to lead hearts he could not win a trick.

Spades are trumps. South leads ◇ 9. East must win and lead another diamond. South trumps with ♠ 4 and North discards ♡ 5. (This play is called a *ruff-and-discard*.) North-South win two of the three tricks. If South had not led the diamond, East-West would have won two tricks.

The Trump Pick-up or Coup

The trump pick-up, or coup, is used when declarer finds (or can infer) that an opponent has a guarded trump honor—but no finesse can be taken because there is no trump card to lead through the opponent. In the end position, when the opponent has nothing but trumps left in his hand, his trump honor can still be picked up by the lead of another suit that he must trump and declarer can overtrump.

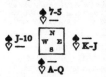

THE TRUMP PICK-UP OR COUP

Hearts are trumps. If there were a heart in the North hand, a finesse could be taken for East's ♡ K-J. North has no hearts, so no finesse is possible. But when a spade is led from the North hand, East must trump and South overtrumps, winning both tricks.

This result is possible only when declarer has no more trumps than the opponent. Often a *trump-reducing play* is necessary: Declarer must arrange

(Continued on next page)

END-PLAYS (Cont'd)

to ruff once or more to reduce the number of his trumps. He may even have to ruff winning cards; when he does this, the play is called the *grand coup*.

The Squeeze

A squeeze occurs when a player who holds stoppers in two or more suits must discard—and cannot discard without relinquishing one of his stoppers. For example:

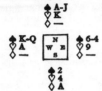

South is declarer; there are no trumps. North-South have only two sure tricks, the ◇ A and ♠ A; West has ♡ A to prevent North's ♡ K from winning a trick, and ♣ K-Q to top the ♠ J. But when South leads ♠ A, West is squeezed: If he discards ♡ A, North discards ♠ J; if he discards ♠ Q, North discards ♡ K. Either way, North-South win all three tricks.

This is the simplest form of the squeeze, which has dozens of variations; but the following rules apply to most of them.

1. One opponent must hold the *only* stoppers in two or more of your suits.

2. You must be able to win *all but one* of the remaining tricks without losing the lead. If you foresee a possible squeeze, you must lose at an early stage of the play whatever tricks must be lost (as by getting an opponent to take his ace in a suit in which you have K-Q-J), until you have all but one of the remaining tricks. This process is called *rectifying the count*.

3. You must have an entry to both partnership hands at the time the squeeze occurs.

THE VIENNA COUP is one of many types of squeeze but is important in bridge legend. Declarer must set up a card in a defender's hand—then squeeze him out of it.

THE VIENNA COUP

There are no trumps. South leads. If South cashed his good spades he would ultimately lose a trick. On the second spade dummy (North) would discard before East and East would discard the same suit. But South first leads ◇ 4 to dummy's ◇ A. This temporarily makes East's ◇ K the master card of its suit. Then South cashes ♠ 8 and ♠ 9, discarding dummy's ◇ 3, and East is squeezed.

```
              ♠ 4
              ♡ A-2
              ◇ A-3
              ♣ —
   ♠ 6-5      N        ♠ 7
   ♡ —      W   E      ♡ K-Q
   ◇ 8-7-6    S        ◇ K-Q
   ♣ —                 ♣ —
              ♠ 9-8
              ♡ 4
              ◇ J-4
              ♣ —
```

CONTRACT BRIDGE LAWS

Contract Bridge is the only card game that has official laws, recognized and used throughout the world. These laws are never revised more often than once in five years and the latest laws, published in 1963, represent the first change since 1948.

The purpose of the laws is to preclude arguments when an irregularity occurs. It is not unsportsmanlike to observe the laws, as is done in all expert games and tournaments.

There are some provisions of the laws that apply to many other laws and to which frequent reference is or could be made in the following pages. They are:

LEAD PENALTY. When declarer may impose a lead penalty he may specify a suit and either require the lead of that suit or forbid the lead of that suit for as long as the opponent retains the lead.*

BARRED PLAYER. A player who is barred once, or for one round, must pass the next time it is his turn to bid; a player who is barred throughout must pass in every turn until the auction of the current deal is completed.

WAIVER OF PENALTY. When a player calls or plays over an illegal call or play by his right-hand opponent, he accepts the illegal call or play and waives a penalty. The game continues as though no irregularity had occurred.

RETENTION OF THE RIGHT TO CALL. A player cannot lose his only chance to call by the fact that an illegal pass by his partner has been accepted by an opponent. The auction must continue until the player has had at least one chance to call.

PENALTY CARD. A card illegally exposed by a defender must be left on the table, face up, until it is played; and it must be played at the first legal opportunity, in leading, following suit, discarding, or trumping. When a defender has a penalty card and his partner has the lead, declarer may require or forbid the partner to lead the suit of the penalty card; but if declarer does so, the card may be picked up and ceases to be a penalty card.

---

*When in the following pages only a "lead penalty" is cited, declarer has these rights. There are some other cases in which declarer has some control over a defender's lead, but not so much. In such cases, the exact penalty will be specified.

DIGEST OF BRIDGE LAWS (Cont'd)

New Shuffle and Cut—Before the first card is dealt, any player may demand a new shuffle and cut. There must be a new shuffle and cut if a card is faced in shuffling or cutting.

Deal Out of Turn—The correct dealer may reclaim the deal before the last card is dealt; thereafter, the deal stands as though it had been in turn and the correct dealer loses his right to deal in that round.

Redeal—There must be a redeal if the cards are not dealt correctly; if the pack is incorrect; if a card is faced in the pack or elsewhere; if a player picks up the wrong hand and looks at it; or if at any time during the play one hand is found to have too many cards and another too few (and the discrepancy is not caused by errors in play). When there is a redeal, the same dealer deals (unless the deal was out of turn) and with the same pack (unless it was imperfect) after a new shuffle and cut.

Incorrect Hand—If a player has too few cards and the missing card is found (except in a previous trick), it is considered to have been in the short hand throughout. If it cannot be found, there is a redeal. If it is found in a previous trick, see *Defective Trick,* page 120.

Enforcing a Penalty—Either opponent (but not dummy) may select or enforce a penalty. If partners consult as to selection or enforcement, the right to penalize is canceled.

Card Exposed During the Auction—No penalty for exposing a single card lower than a ten. If the exposed card is an honor, or any card prematurely led, or more than one card, each exposed card must be left face up on the table; the partner of the offender must pass at his next turn; and each exposed card becomes a penalty card if the other side plays the hand.

Change of Call—A player may change a call without penalty if he does so without pause. Any other attempted change of call is canceled. If the first call was an illegal call, it is subject to the applicable law; if it was a legal call, the offender may either:

(a) allow his first call to stand, whereupon his partner must pass at his next turn; or

(b) substitute any legal call (including a pass, double, or redouble) whereupon his partner must pass at every subsequent turn.

DIGEST OF BRIDGE LAWS (Cont'd)

Insufficient Bid—If a player makes an insufficient bid, he must substitute either a sufficient bid or a pass (not a double or redouble). If he substitutes:

(a) The lowest sufficient bid in the same denomination, there is no penalty.

(b) Any other bid, his partner must pass at every subsequent turn.

(c) A pass, his partner must pass at every subsequent turn, and declarer (if an opponent) may impose a lead penalty (page 114). A double or redouble illegally substituted is penalized the same as a pass and is treated as a pass.

The offender need not select his final call until the law has been stated; previous attempts at correction are canceled.

Information Given in Changing Call—A denomination named, then canceled, in making or correcting an illegal call, is subject to penalty if an opponent becomes declarer: if a suit was named, declarer may impose a lead penalty (page 114); if notrump was named, declarer may call a suit, if the offender's partner has the opening lead; if a double or redouble was canceled, the penalties are the same as when a pass is substituted for an insufficient bid.

Call out of Rotation (or "out of turn")—Any call out of rotation is canceled when attention is drawn to it. The auction reverts to the player whose turn it was. Rectification and penalty depend on whether it was a pass, a bid, or a double or redouble, as follows.

A call is not out of rotation if made without waiting for the right-hand opponent to pass, if that opponent is legally obliged to pass; nor if it would have been in rotation had not the left-hand opponent called out of rotation. A call made simultaneously with another player's call in rotation is deemed to be subsequent to it.

Pass out of Turn—If it occurs (a) before any player has bid, or when it was the turn of the offender's right-hand opponent, the offender must pass when his regular turn comes; (b) after there has been a bid and when it was the turn of the offender's partner, the offender is barred throughout; the offender's partner may not double or redouble at that turn; and if the offender's partner passes and the opponents play the hand, declarer may impose a lead penalty (page 114).

Bid out of Turn—If it occurs (a) before any player has called, the offender's partner is barred through-

DIGEST OF BRIDGE LAWS (Cont'd)

out; (b) after any player has called and when it was the turn of the offender's partner, the offender's partner is barred throughout and is subject to a lead penalty (page 114) if he has the opening lead; (c) after any player has called and when it was the turn of the offender's right-hand opponent, the offender must repeat his bid without penalty if that opponent passes but if that opponent bids the offender may make any call and his partner is barred once.

Double or Redouble out of Turn—If it occurs (a) when it was the turn of the offender's partner, the offender's partner is barred throughout and is subject to a lead penalty (page 114) if he has the opening lead, and the offender may not in turn double or redouble the same bid; (b) when it was the turn of the offender's right-hand opponent, the offender must repeat his double or redouble without penalty if that opponent passes but may make any legal call if that opponent bids, in which case the offender's partner is barred once.

Impossible Doubles and Redoubles—If a player doubles or redoubles a bid that his side has already doubled or redoubled, his call is canceled; he must substitute (a) any legal bid, in which case his partner is barred throughout and if he becomes the opening leader declarer may prohibit the lead of the doubled suit; or (b) a pass, in which case either opponent may cancel all previous doubles and redoubles, the offender's partner is barred throughout, and if he becomes the opening leader he is subject to a lead penalty (page 114).

If a player doubles his partner's bid, redoubles an undoubled bid, or doubles or redoubles when there has been no bid, he must substitute any proper call, and his partner is barred once.

Other Inadmissible Calls—If a player bids more than seven, or makes another call when legally required to pass, he is deemed to have passed and the offending side must pass at every subsequent turn; if they become the defenders, declarer may impose a lead penalty (page 114) on the opening leader.

Call After the Auction is Closed—A call made after the auction is closed is canceled. If it is a pass by a defender, or any call by declarer or dummy, there is no penalty. If it is a bid, double or redouble by a defender, declarer may impose a lead penalty at the offender's partner's first turn to lead.

Dummy's Rights—Dummy may give or obtain in-

POINT-COUNT VALUATION

BIDDABLE SUITS

OPENING ONE-BIDS

CHOICE OF SUITS

FORCING BIDS

RESPONSES TO SUIT-BIDS

OPENER'S REBIDS

RESPONDER'S REBIDS

NOTRUMP BIDDING

OPENING 3, 4, 5 BIDS

FORCING TWO-BIDS

OVERCALLS

TAKEOUT DOUBLE

PENALTY DOUBLES

PART-SCORE

DUPLICATE

SLAM BIDS

4-5 NOTRUMP SLAM BIDS

BIDDING CONVENTIONS

PERCENTAGE TABLES

BIDDING SYSTEMS

OPENING LEADS

SIGNALS IN PLAY

COVERING HONORS

FINESSES

SAFETY PLAYS

END-PLAYS SQUEEZE

BRIDGE LAWS

GLOSSARY

formation regarding fact or law, ask if a play constitutes a revoke, draw attention to an irregularity, and warn any player against infringing a law. Dummy forfeits these rights if he looks at a card in another player's hand.

If dummy has forfeited his rights, and thereafter (a) is the first to draw attention to a defender's irregularity, declarer may not enforce any penalty for the offense; (b) warns declarer not to lead from the wrong hand, either defender may choose the hand from which declarer shall lead; (c) is the first to ask declarer if a play from declarer's hand is a revoke, declarer must correct a revoke if able but the revoke penalty still applies.

Exposed Cards—Declarer is never subject to penalty for exposure of a card, but intentional exposure of declarer's hand is treated as a claim or concession of tricks.

A defender's card is exposed if it is faced on the table or held so that the other defender may see its face before he is entitled to do so. Such a card must be left face up on the table until played and becomes a penalty card.

Penalty Cards—A penalty card must be played at the first legal opportunity, subject to the obligation to follow suit or to comply with another penalty.

If a defender has two or more penalty cards that he can legally play, declarer may designate which one is to be played.

Declarer may require or forbid a defender to lead a suit in which his partner has a penalty card, but if declarer does so the penalty card may be picked up and ceases to be a penalty card.

Failure to play a penalty card is not subject to penalty, but declarer may require the penalty card to be played and any defender's card exposed in the process becomes a penalty card.

Lead Out of Turn—If declarer is required by a defender* to retract a lead from the wrong hand, he must lead from the correct hand (if he can) a card of the same suit; if it was a defender's turn to lead, or if there is no card of that suit in the correct hand, there is no penalty.

If a defender is required to retract a lead out of turn, declarer may either treat the card so led as a penalty card, or impose a lead penalty on the offender's partner when next he is to lead after the offense.

---

*A defender's drawing attention to declarer's lead from the wrong hand is equivalent to requiring its retraction.

DIGEST OF BRIDGE LAWS (Cont'd)

Premature Play—If a defender leads to the next trick before his partner has played to the current trick, or plays out of rotation before his partner has played, declarer may require the offender's partner to play his highest card of the suit led, his lowest card of the suit led, or a card of another specified suit. Declarer must select one of these options and if the defender cannot comply, he may play any card. When declarer has played from both his hand and dummy, a defender is not subject to penalty for playing before his partner.

Inability to Play as Required—If a player is unable to lead or play as required to comply with a penalty (for lack of a card of a required suit, or because of the prior obligation to follow suit) he may play any card. The penalty is deemed satisfied, except in the case of a penalty card.

Revoke—A revoke is the act of playing a card of another suit, when able to follow suit to a lead. Any player, including dummy, may ask whether a play constitutes a revoke and may demand that an opponent correct a revoke. A claim of revoke does not warrant inspection of turned tricks, prior to the end of play, except by consent of both sides.

Correcting a Revoke—A player must correct his revoke if aware of it before it becomes established. A revoke card withdrawn by a defender becomes a penalty card. The nonoffending side may withdraw any cards played after the revoke but before attention was drawn to it.

Established Revoke—A revoke becomes established when a member of the offending side leads or plays to a subsequent trick (or terminates play by a claim or concession). When a revoke becomes established, the revoke trick stands as played (unless it is the twelfth trick—see below).

Revoke Penalty—The penalty for an established revoke is two tricks (if available), transferred at the end of play from the revoking side to the opponents. This penalty can be paid only from tricks won by the revoking side after its first revoke, including the revoke trick. If only one trick is available, the penalty is satisfied by transferring one trick; if no trick is available, there is no penalty.

There is no penalty for a subsequent established revoke in the same suit by the same player.

A transferred trick ranks for all scoring purposes

DIGEST OF BRIDGE LAWS (Cont'd)

as a trick won in play by the side receiving it. It never affects the contract.*

Revokes Not Subject to Penalty—A revoke made in the twelfth trick must be corrected, without penalty, if discovered before the cards have been mixed together. The nonoffending side may require the offender's partner to play either of two cards he could legally have played. A revoke not discovered until the cards have been mixed is not subject to penalty, nor is a revoke by any faced hand (dummy, or a defender's hand when faced in consequence of a claim by declarer). A revoke by failure to play a penalty card is not subject to the penalty for an established revoke.

Defective Trick—A defective trick may not be corrected after a player of each side has played to the next trick. If a player has failed to play to a trick, he must correct his error when it is discovered by adding a card to the trick (if possible, one he could legally have played to it). If a player has played more than one card to a trick, he does not play to the last trick or tricks and if he wins a trick with his last card, the turn to lead passes to the player at his left.

Declarer Claiming or Conceding Tricks—If declarer claims or concedes one or more of the remaining tricks (verbally or by spreading his hand), he must leave his hand face up on the table and immediately state his intended plan of play.

If a defender disputes declarer's claim, declarer must play on, adhering to any statement he has made, and in the absence of a specific statement he may not "exercise freedom of choice in making any play the success of which depends on finding either opponent with or without a particular unplayed card."

Following curtailment of play by declarer, it is permissible for a defender to expose his hand and to suggest a play to his partner.

Defender Claiming or Conceding Tricks—A defender may show any or all of his cards to declarer to establish a claim or concession. He may not expose his hand to his partner, and if he does, declarer may treat his partner's cards as penalty cards.

Correcting the Score—A proved or admitted error in any score may be corrected at any time before

---

*For example, if the contract is 2 ♡ and declarer wins 8 tricks plus 2 tricks as a revoke penalty, total 10 tricks, he can score only 60 points below the line and the other 60 points go above the line.

DIGEST OF BRIDGE LAWS (Cont'd)

the rubber score is agreed, except as follows. An error made in entering or failing to enter a part-score, or in omitting a game or in awarding one, may not be corrected after the last card of the second succeeding correct deal has been dealt (unless a majority of the players consent).

Effect of Incorrect Pack—Scores made as a result of hands played with an incorrect pack are not affected by the discovery of the imperfection after the cards have been mixed together.

FOUR-DEAL BRIDGE
Also called Chicago or Club Bridge

This is a popular form of bridge in clubs because a player does not have to wait more than 20 minutes to cut into a game.

Four deals constitute a rubber. On the first deal, neither side is vulnerable; on the second and third deals, dealer's side is vulnerable and the other side is not; on the fourth deal both sides are vulnerable.

There is a bonus of 300 for making a nonvulnerable game and 500 for making a vulnerable game. On the fourth deal there is a bonus of 100 for making a part-score that does not complete a game. Tricks, penalties, slams and honors are scored as in rubber bridge but there is no rubber bonus. Part-scores carry over, but any game wipes out previous part-scores.

A deal passed out does not count; the same dealer deals again.

A deal out of turn that is not detected in time (page 115) does not affect the right of the player who should have dealt to call first; but if the first call is made by the player who actually dealt the cards, there is no penalty; the auction continues as though he should have called first; but the position of the player who should have dealt still determines the vulnerability on that deal.

A fifth or subsequent deal is void if attention is drawn to it before the next deal has been completed (or the game has broken up). If it is too late to void the deal, it is scored with neither side vulnerable.

The "wheel" is used on the score sheet to keep track of who dealt first and the rotation of the deal and vulnerability. The scorekeeper writes "1" in the position of the first dealer, then successively "2," "3," "4," as each successive dealer's turn comes. In this diagram, the player at the scorekeeper's right dealt first, the scorekeeper is dealing or has dealt, and the scorekeeper will write "3" in the next space as it becomes the turn of the player at his left to deal.

POINT-COUNT VALUATION

BIDDABLE SUITS

OPENING ONE-BIDS

CHOICE OF SUITS

FORCING BIDS

RESPONSES TO SUIT-BIDS

OPENER'S REBIDS

RESPONDER'S REBIDS

NOTRUMP BIDDING

OPENING 3, 4, 5 BIDS

FORCING TWO-BIDS

OVERCALLS

TAKEOUT DOUBLE

PENALTY DOUBLES

PART-SCORE

DUPLICATE

SLAM BIDS

4-5 NOTRUMP SLAM BIDS

BIDDING CONVENTIONS

PERCENTAGE TABLES

BIDDING SYSTEMS

OPENING LEADS

SIGNALS IN PLAY

COVERING HONORS

FINESSES

SAFETY PLAYS

END-PLAYS SQUEEZE

BRIDGE LAWS

GLOSSARY

GLOSSARY

Above the Line: Not counting toward game.

Adequate Trump Support: The minimum holding in partner's suit that justifies raising it.

Auction: (1) All the calls made by the four players. (2) The period of time beginning at the conclusion of the deal² and ending when a call made by one player is followed by three passes in rotation.

Balance: Reopen the bidding, relying on strength assumed to be in partner's hand because the opponents have stopped at a low contract.

Balanced Hand: A hand containing no void or singleton.

Bare: (1) To discard the last guard of (a high card). (2) Unguarded; alone.

Barred: Required to pass, in consequence of a penalty.

Bath Coup: The play of ducking the lead of a king when holding A-J-x.

Below the Line: Counting toward game.

Bid: An undertaking to win a specified number of tricks in a denomination (trump or notrump) named in the bid.

Business Double: A penalty double.

Call: A bid, double, redouble, or pass.

Cash: To lead (one or more winning cards).

Come-on: An encouraging or high-low signal by a defender.

Contract: (1) The game of Contract Bridge. (2) The final legal bid made during the auction, whether undoubled, doubled, or redoubled.

Convention: A call or play having a definitely understood meaning, usually based on the logic of the bidding or playing situation.

Cooperative Double: An optional double.

Coup: (1) Any master stroke or brilliant play. (2) A trump pick-up.

Cover: To play a higher card than (the highest previously played to a trick).

Cross-ruff: To ruff alternately in one hand of the partnership and the other.

Cue-bid: A bid designed to show the ace (or a void) in the suit bid.

Culbertson System: The bidding system most popular c. 1930-49, replaced by the similar Goren System described in this book.

Deal: (1) A complete deck of 52 cards divided into four hands of 13 cards each. (2) The period of time during which a deal is in play. (3) The distribution of the cards in rotation to the players.

Declarer: The player who for his side plays both his own and the dummy hands.

Defender: In play, an opponent of declarer; in bidding, a member of the side that does not make the first bid.

Defending Hand: A defender.

Defensive Trick: An honor-trick or other card that will probably win a trick even if an opponent becomes declarer.

Deschapelles Coup: The sacrifice lead of a king to give partner an entry.

Discard: To play a card of a suit other than the suit led and the trump suit.

Distribution: (1) The manner in which the 13 cards of a suit are divided among the four players. (2) The hand-pattern or the manner in which the four suits are divided in a single player's hand. (3) The four hand-patterns of any deal or the manner in which the 52 cards are divided among the four players.

Double: A call that increases certain scoring values if the last preceding bid becomes the contract. A player may double only if the last bid was made by an opponent and no call other than a pass has intervened.

Doubleton: An original holding of two cards in a suit.

Down: Defeated at one's contract.

Dummy: (1) The hand of declarer's partner after the opening lead. (2) Declarer's partner.

Dummy Reversal: Use by declarer of his own, longer, trump suit for ruffing and of dummy's shorter trump suit to draw trumps.

Duplicate Bridge: A method of playing bridge in which competing pairs hold the same cards, play them against different opponents, and compare their respective scores.

Entry: A card that wins a trick, giving the lead to the winning hand.

Equals: Two cards of adjacent rank in the same suit.

Established Suit: A suit in which neither opponent holds a winning card.

False-card: A card played with the intention of deceiving the adversaries as to one's true holding.

Fillers: Tens, nines, etc., not counted in points, which increase the general strength of a player's hand.

Finesse: Play (of) a card lower than one's highest card of the same suit, in the hope that any card of intervening rank is held by an opponent who has already played to the trick.

Follow Suit: To play a card of the suit led.

Force: (1) A call that requires partner to keep the bidding open. (2) To lead a card that declarer must ruff to avoid losing a trick.

Forcing Bid: A bid that conventionally demands that partner keep the bidding open.

Forcing Pass: A pass of an opponent's bid in a situation in which partner is expected to bid or double.

Forcing Rebid: A jump bid in a

GLOSSARY (Cont'd)

new suit by a player who has previously bid.

Forcing Takeout: A jump response in a new suit by a player who has not previously called.

Four Aces System: A bidding system used by a team of the greatest American players *c.* 1934-48, employing a 3-2-1-½ point-count, the source of many modern methods.

Fourth Hand: The last player in turn to bid.

Freak: A hand containing eleven or more cards in two suits; or one suit of eight or more cards.

Free Bid, Raise or Response: A bid, raise or response made immediately over a bid by the right-hand opponent.

Game: A trick-score of 100 points or more, made in one or more deals uninterrupted by an opponent's game.

Guard: A card of a suit in which a player holds one or more higher cards.

Hand: (1) The 13 cards held by one player during a deal, or any part thereof remaining unplayed. (2) One of the four players. (3) Same as deal[1].

Honor-score: Points scored above the line.

Honor-trick: A card or combination of cards that can be expected to win a trick by virtue of its rank; a quick trick.

Informatory Double: A takeout double.

Jump Bid: A bid higher than necessary to overcall the last preceding bid.

Jump Trump Rebid or Response: An unnecessary jump bid in a suit, following an opening two-bid, a forcing takeout, or a forcing rebid, to show a nearly solid suit.

Karpin Point-count: A form of the 4-3-2-1 point-count, used by many authorities, by which distributional points are counted for long suits rather than short suits.

Keep the Bidding Open: Make a call other than a pass, if a pass would permit an opponent to close the auction by passing.

Lead: (1) To play the first card to a trick. (2) The card so led.

Length: A holding of four or more cards of a suit.

Level: The number of odd-tricks in the current bid.

Long Card: An unplayed card of a suit whose other cards have all been played.

Long Suit: A holding of four or more cards in a suit. Also, length.

Loser: A card that may be lost to the opponents during the play. Also, losing trick.

Major Suit: Either the spade or the heart suit.

Match-point: The scoring unit in certain types of duplicate bridge.

Each match-point signifies the defeat of one contesting pair on one deal.

Minor Suit: Either the diamond or the club suit.

Negative Double: (1) A takeout double. (2) A Roth-Stone or responsive double.

New Suit: A suit that has not previously been bid during the auction of the deal in progress.

Odd-even Discards: A defender's signaling convention whereby an odd-numbered small card (as, 3, 5, 7, 9) is encouraging and an even-numbered card discouraging, used in the Roman Club System.

Odd-trick: Each trick won by declarer in excess of six.

Opener: The player who makes the first bid. Also, opening hand.

Optional Double: A double of a preëmptive bid, inviting partner to bid or pass, depending on his hand.

Overbid: A contract that cannot or should not be fulfilled.

Overcall: (1) A bid made by a defender. (2) To make a bid that is higher in rank than (an opponent's bid).

Over-ruff: To play a higher trump than one previously played as a ruff to the same trick.

Overtrick: Each odd-trick won by declarer in excess of his contract.

Overtrump: Over-ruff.

Partners: Two persons playing together for a common score.

Part-score: (1) A contract of less than game. (2) The points earned for making such a contract.

Pass: A call signifying that the player is not at that time bid, double, or redouble.

Penalty: (1) Points scored above the line by the defenders for defeating the contract. (2) Any disability imposed on a player for a violation of a law of the game.

Penalty Double: A double made in the expectation of defeating the opponents' contract.

Pip: A suit-designating symbol, ♠, ♡, ◇, or ♣.

Play: (1) The period during which the cards are played in a series of tricks. This period begins when the auction closes and ends when the number of tricks won by each side is agreed upon. (2) To lead, follow suit, trump, or discard.

Playing Trick: See winner.

Position: The place occupied by a player or by a card at the bridge table, especially with respect to other players or cards.

Preemptive Bid: A shut-out bid.

Protection: A bid made to reopen the bidding, in the belief that partner has passed a strong hand.

Psychic: A bid made for psychological effect, not justifiable by the values in the hand but designed to mislead the opponents.

POINT-COUNT VALUATION

BIDDABLE SUITS

OPENING ONE-BIDS

CHOICE OF SUITS

FORCING BIDS

RESPONSES TO SUIT-BIDS

OPENER'S REBIDS

RESPONDER'S REBIDS

NOTRUMP BIDDING

OPENING 3, 4, 5 BIDS

FORCING TWO-BIDS

OVERCALLS

TAKEOUT DOUBLE

PENALTY DOUBLES

PART-SCORE

DUPLICATE

SLAM BIDS

4-5 NOTRUMP SLAM BIDS

BIDDING CONVENTIONS

PERCENTAGE TABLES

BIDDING SYSTEMS

OPENING LEADS

SIGNALS IN PLAY

COVERING HONORS

FINESSES

SAFETY PLAYS

END-PLAYS SQUEEZE

BRIDGE LAWS

GLOSSARY

Quick Trick: A high card or card-combination, such as an Ace or K-Q, that will probably win a trick the first or second time its suit is led.

Raise: (1) To support partner's bid. (2) An increase of partner's bid at the same denomination by one or more odd-tricks.

Rebid: The second or any subsequent bid made by a player.

Rectify the Count: Lose a trick intentionally to prepare for a squeeze.

Redouble: A call that further increases certain scoring values established by a double. A player may redouble only if the last preceding call, other than a pass, was a double by an opponent.

Reith or New England Count: A point count, 6-4-3-2-1 (for a ten), still used by many players.

Responder: The partner of the player who made the opening bid or who made any call (such as a takeout double) that requests a response.

Response: A call other than a pass made by the partner of a player who in his previous turn has made a bid.

Responsive double: (1) A double in response to partner's takeout double. (2) A negative double.

Revoke: Failure to follow suit when able to do so.

Rotation: The order (from each player to the player at his left) in which the distribution of cards in the deal, the turns to call, and the turns to play to a lead, progress. This order is clockwise.

Rubber: A series of deals beginning when it is determined which pairs of the four players will be partners, and ending when a side has won two games.

Ruff: To play a trump when some other suit has been led.

Run: To lead (the cards of an established suit).

Rusinow Leads: The conventional lead of K from A-K, Q from K-Q, J from Q-J, 10 from J-10, instead of the traditional lead of the higher card.

Sacrifice: A deliberate overbid made with the intention of paying a penalty rather than permit the opponents to obtain the contract.

Sequence: Three or more cards in consecutive order of rank, when held by the same player.

Set: To defeat (the opponents' contract).

Shut-out: An unnecessarily high bid, designed to make it difficult for the other side to enter the auction.

Side: The partnership of two players.

Side Suit: A suit that is not the trump suit.

Sign-off: Any of various bids that show weakness and ask partner to pass.

Singleton: An original holding of only one card in a suit.

Slam: A contract to take all or all but one of the tricks. The former is a *grand slam*; the latter, a *small slam* or *little slam*.

Solid: Said of a suit that can be established by straight leads (as, Q-J-10-9-x-x), or of a suit in which no trick need be lost (as, A-K-Q-J-x-x).

Squeeze: A play that forces an opponent to discard a card which if retained would win a trick.

Standard American System: A term designating the general bidding principles to which most players in North America adhere, but with modifications to suit individual preferences: the system on which this book is essentially based, now best exemplified by the Goren System and previously by the Culbertson System.

Stopper: A card or combination of cards that can be expected to win a trick in the opponents' strong suit.

Takeout: (1) A response in a denomination other than that which one's partner has bid. (2) Intended to be taken out by partner, as a *takeout double*.

Tenace: Two cards separated in rank by one or two cards held by the opponents.

Third Hand: The third player in turn to bid or play.

Top of nothing: An opening lead of the highest of three low cards, as the eight from 8-5-2.

Touching: Consecutive in rank.

Trick: Four cards, one played from each hand. A trick begins with the lead; it is completed when each hand has played one card to it.

Trick Score: The point value of odd-tricks in a contract fulfilled.

Trump: (1) See *trump suit*. (2) To play a trump when another suit was led.

Trump Suit: The suit, if any, named in the contract. Each of its cards is a trump and ranks above any card of any other suit.

Unbalanced Hand: A hand containing a void or singleton.

Undertrick: Each trick by which declarer falls short of the number required by the contract.

Unguard: To discard an essential guard of (a high card).

Void: An original holding of no card in a suit.

Vulnerable: Having won a game.

Winner: A card that wins a trick or may be expected to win a trick.

x: In bridge notation, any card lower than the holder's lowest specified card; it must be a card whose rank can have no effect on the winning of tricks.

Yarborough: A hand containing no card as high as a ten.

HOW TO FIND YOUR BEST BID, LEAD OR PLAY

CONTRACT BRIDGE SCORING TABLE

TRICK-SCORE (scored below the line)

If trumps are	♣	♦	♡	♠	NT	
For each trick over six bid and made, undoubled	20	20	30	30	40	(1st trick)
					30	(each subsequent trick)

If contract is doubled, multiply by 2; if redoubled, by 4.

PREMIUMS (scored above the line)

For winning RUBBER, if opponents have no game.....................700
For winning RUBBER, if opponents have a game....................500
For having one game in an unfinished rubber.........................300
For having a part-score (or scores) in an unfinished game.............. 50

For four trump HONORS (A, K, Q, J, 10) in one hand.................100
For five trump HONORS, or four aces at notrump, in one hand.........150

For making a SLAM	Not Vulnerable	Vulnerable
Small Slam (12 tricks bid and made).......	500	750
Grand Slam (13 tricks bid and made).......	1000	1500

For each OVERTRICK (won but not bid for)	Not Vulnerable Trick Value	Vulnerable Trick Value
If undoubled	Trick Value	Trick Value
Doubled	100	200
Redoubled	200	400
For making any doubled or redoubled contract	50	50

For UNDERTRICKS (tricks by which opponents fall short of their contract)	Not Vulnerable		Vulnerable	
	Undoubled	Doubled	Undoubled	Doubled
1 Down....................	50	100	100	200
2 Down....................	100	300	200	500
3 Down....................	150	500	300	800
4 Down....................	200	700	400	1100
5 Down....................	250	900	500	1400
Each additional trick ADDS..	50	200	100	300
When contract is redoubled, multiply doubled value by 2.				

First side to score 100 points below the line, in one or more hands, wins a GAME. When a game is won, both sides start scoreless toward the next game. First side to win two games wins the RUBBER.

INTERNATIONAL MATCH-POINTS

Difference in points	*I.M.P.*	*Difference in points*	*I.M.P.*	*Difference in points*	*I.M.P.*	*Difference in points*	*IM.P.*
20– 40	1	270–310	7	750– 890	13	2000–2240	19
50– 80	2	320–360	8	900–1090	14	2250–2490	20
90–120	3	370–420	9	1100–1290	15	2500–2990	21
130–160	4	430–490	10	1300–1490	16	3000–3490	22
170–210	5	500–590	11	1500–1740	17	3500–3990	23
220–260	6	600–740	12	1750–1990	18	4000 & up	24